Hormone Helper

Les Christie

Stan Campbell

David C. Cook Publishing Co.
Elgin, Illinois—Weston, Ontario

Custom Curriculum
Hormone Helper

Unless otherwise noted, Scripture quotations are from the Holy Bible, New International Version (NIV), © 1973, 1978, 1984 by International Bible Society. Used by permission of Zondervan Bible Publishers.

Published by David C. Cook Publishing Co.
850 North Grove Ave., Elgin, IL 60120
Cable address: DCCOOK
Series creator: John Duckworth
Series editor: Randy Southern
Editor: Randy Southern
Option writers: John Duckworth, Nelson E. Copeland, Jr., and Ellen Larson
Designer: Bill Paetzold
Cover illustrator: Mitch O'Connell
Inside illustrator: Al Hering
Printed in U.S.A.

ISBN: 0-7814-5004-7

CONTENTS

Sessions by Stan Campbell
Options by John Duckworth, Nelson E. Copeland, Jr., and Ellen Larson

About the Authors

Stan Campbell has been a youth worker for over eighteen years, and has written several books on youth ministry including the *BibleLog* series (SonPower) and the *Quick Studies* series (David C. Cook). He and his wife, Pam, are youth directors at Lisle Bible Church in Lisle, Illinois.

John Duckworth is a writer and illustrator in Carol Stream, Illinois. He has worked with teenagers in youth groups and Sunday school, written several books including *The School Zone* (SonPower), and created such youth resources as *Hot Topics Youth Electives* and *Snap Sessions* for David C. Cook.

Nelson E. Copeland, Jr. is a nationally known speaker and the author of several youth resources including *Great Games for City Kids* (Youth Specialties) and *A New Agenda for Urban Youth* (Winston-Derek). He is president of the Christian Education Coalition for African-American Leadership (CECAAL), an organization dedicated to reinforcing educational and cultural excellence among urban teenagers. He also serves as youth pastor at the First Baptist Church in Morton, Pennsylvania.

Ellen Larson is an educator and writer with degrees in education and theology. She has served as minister of Christian education in several churches, teaching teens and children, as well as their teachers. Her experience also includes teaching in public schools. She is the author of several books for Christian education teachers, and frequently leads training seminars for volunteer teachers. Ellen and her husband live in San Diego and are the parents of two daughters.

You've Made the Right Choice!

Thanks for choosing **Custom Curriculum**! We think your choice says at least three things about you:

(1) You know your group pretty well, and want your program to fit that group like a glove;

(2) You like having options instead of being boxed in by some far-off curriculum editor;

(3) You have a small mole on your left forearm, exactly two inches above the elbow.

OK, so we were wrong about the mole. But if you like having choices that help you tailor meetings to fit your kids, **Custom Curriculum** *is* the best place to be.

Going through Customs

In this (and every) **Custom Curriculum** volume, you'll find
• five great sessions you can use anytime, in any order.
• reproducible student handouts, at least one per session.
• a truckload of options for adapting the sessions to your group (more about that in a minute).
• a helpful get-you-ready article by a youth expert.
• clip art for making posters, fliers, and other kinds of publicity to get kids to your meetings.

Each **Custom Curriculum** session has three to six steps. No matter how many steps a session has, it's designed to achieve these goals:

• *Getting together.* Using an icebreaker activity, you'll help kids be glad they came to the meeting.

• *Getting thirsty.* Why should kids care about your topic? Why should they care what the Bible has to say about it? You'll want to take a few minutes to earn their interest before you start pouring the "living water."

• *Getting the Word.* By exploring and discussing carefully selected passages, you'll find out what God has to say.

• *Getting the point.* Here's where you'll help kids make the leap from principles to nitty-gritty situations they are likely to face.

• *Getting personal.* What should each group member do as a result of this session? You'll help each person find a specific "next-step" response that works for him or her.

Each session is written to last 45 to 60 minutes. But what if you have less time—or more? No problem! **Custom Curriculum** is all about ... options!

What Are My Options?

Every **Custom Curriculum** session gives you fourteen kinds of options:

• *Extra Action*—for groups that learn better when they're physically moving (instead of just reading, writing, and discussing).

• *Combined Junior High/High School*—to use when you're mixing age levels, and an activity or case study would be too "young" or "old" for part of the group.

• *Small Group*—for adapting activities that would be tough with groups of fewer than eight kids.

• *Large Group*—to alter steps for groups of more than twenty kids.

• *Urban*—for fitting sessions to urban facilities and multiethnic (especially African-American) concerns.

• *Heard It All Before*—for fresh approaches that get past the defenses of kids who are jaded by years in church.

• *Little Bible Background*—to use when most of your kids are strangers to the Bible, or haven't made a Christian commitment.

• *Mostly Guys*—to focus on guys' interests and to substitute activities they might be more enthused about.

• *Mostly Girls*—to address girls' concerns and to substitute activities they might prefer.

• *Extra Fun*—for longer, more "rowdy" youth meetings where the emphasis is on fun.

• *Short Meeting Time*—tips for condensing the session to 30 minutes or so.

• *Fellowship & Worship*—for building deeper relationships or enabling kids to praise God together.

• *Media*—to spice up meetings with video, music, or other popular media.

• *Sixth Grade*—appearing only in junior high/middle school volumes, this option helps you change steps that sixth graders might find hard to understand or relate to.

• *Extra Challenge*—appearing only in high school volumes, this option lets you crank up the voltage for kids who are ready for more Scripture or more demanding personal application.

Each kind of option is offered twice in each session. So in this book, you get *almost 150* ways to tweak the meetings to fit your group!

Customizing a Session

All right, you may be thinking. *With all of these options flying around, how do I put a session together? I don't have a lot of time, you know.*

We know! That's why we've made **Custom Curriculum** as easy to follow as possible. Let's take a look at how you might prepare an actual meeting. You can do that in four easy steps:

(1) *Read the basic session plan.* Start by choosing one or more of the goals listed at the beginning of the session. You have three to pick from: a goal that emphasizes *knowledge,* one that stresses *understanding,* and one that emphasizes *action.* Choose one or more, depending on what *you* want to accomplish. Then read the basic plan to see what will work for you and what might not.

(2) *Choose your options.* You don't *have* to use any options at all; the

basic session plan would work well for many groups, and you may want to stick with it if you have absolutely no time to consider options. But if you want a more perfect fit, check out your choices.

As you read the basic session plan, you'll see small symbols in the margin. Each symbol stands for a different kind of option. When you see a symbol, it means that kind of option is offered for that step. Turn to the page noted by the symbol and you'll see that option explained.

Let's say you have a small group, mostly guys who get bored if they don't keep moving. You'll want to keep an eye out for three kinds of options: Small Group, Mostly Guys, and Extra Action. As you read the basic session, you might spot symbols that tell you there are Small Group options for Step 1 and Step 3—maybe a different way to play a game so that you don't need big teams, and a way to cover several Bible passages when just a few kids are looking them up. Then you see symbols telling you that there are Mostly Guys options for Step 2 and Step 4—perhaps a substitute activity that doesn't require too much self-disclosure, and a case study guys will relate to. Finally you see symbols indicating Extra Action options for Step 2 and Step 3—maybe an active way to get kids' opinions instead of handing out a survey, and a way to act out some verses instead of just looking them up.

After reading the options, you might decide to use four of them. You base your choices on your personal tastes and the traits of your group that you think are most important right now. **Custom Curriculum** offers you more options than you'll need, so you can pick your current favorites and plug others into future meetings if you like.

(3) *Use the checklist.* Once you've picked your options, keep track of them with the simple checklist that appears at the end of each option section (just before the start of the next session plan). This little form gives you a place to write down the materials you'll need too—since they depend on the options you've chosen.

(4) *Get your stuff together.* Gather your materials; photocopy any Repro Resources (reproducible student sheets) you've decided to use. And … you're ready!

The Custom Curriculum Challenge

Your kids are fortunate to have you as their leader. You see them not as a bunch of generic teenagers, but as real, live, unique kids. You care whether you really connect with them. That's why you're willing to take a few extra minutes to tailor your meetings to fit.

It's a challenge to work with real, live kids, isn't it? We think you deserve a standing ovation for taking that challenge. And we pray that **Custom Curriculum** helps you shape sessions that shape lives for Jesus Christ and His kingdom.

—The Editors

Talking to Kids about Sex

by Les Christie

I speak to thousands of young people each year about sex and I'm still shocked by the statistics:

• Twelve million teens are sexually active.

• Eight out of ten males and seven out of ten females report having had intercourse while in their teens.

• If present trends continue, forty percent of today's fourteen-year-old girls will be pregnant at least once before the age of twenty.

• Fifty percent of all sexually active nineteen-year-old males had their first sexual experience between the ages of eleven and thirteen.

• By senior year of high school, one in four high school students have had at least four sex partners.

Unfortunately, many young people receive their sex education from the media. The average high school student had the opportunity to watch 14,000 acts of intercourse or innuendo to intercourse on prime time TV in 1991. He or she will watch an average of ten hours a week of MTV.

However, more unfortunate than the media's influence is the fact that only about 10% of young people today receive good, positive, healthy Christian sex education. It is unfortunate that parents and the church have remained more or less silent when it comes to sex education. Sexuality isn't an easy subject to discuss with our kids, but our silence is hurting this generation of young people who desire to hear the truth.

By discussing sexuality with your young people, you may prevent some very negative experiences. You will also be giving the gift of a healthy attitude and godly stewardship of one of God's most special gifts to us, our sexuality.

Tips on Getting Started

As you work through these sessions in *Hormone Helper*, get in touch with the feelings you had about sexuality when you were in high school. How did you feel and what were you thinking about on your first date, your first kiss, the first time you had to say "no," or a time you said "yes" and regretted it?

Also you'll need to keep parents informed. If the parents of your group members aren't kept up-to-date on your plans, your efforts will be wasted. Let parents know what material you will be covering. Send them portions of the material or extra material so they can follow up in their homes. Design questions for parents to discuss with their kids after the *Hormone Helper* series. Most parents feel the weight of responsibility for the sex education of their kids, but do not feel adequate for the task. They are usually grateful when any kind of program is offered in a Christian context.

Over the years, I've faced three areas of objections to having a series on love, sex, and dating. The first objection is that kids are faced with too much sexual information already, and don't need to hear more of it in a church or youth group setting. However, that's the *reason* for this study. Young people need sound, biblical information, not locker-room talk. The second objection is that there are too many controversial issues involved in sex education. This is a valid point; however, there are some absolutes in Scripture. Even the questionable areas—masturbation, premarital petting, contraception—need to be discussed. The third objection goes something like this: "*We didn't have a course on sex, and we turned out all right*—so our kids can too." The problem with this argument is that not everyone was a "survivor." Many people did not "turn out all right." For many people, a lack of sex education did irreparable damage to their lives. Besides, it's unfair to compare the teens of today with the teens of previous generations. Teens today face *much* more sexual pressure and confusion than even the teens of only one generation ago. Teens of the 90s desperately need help, encouragement, and positive support.

I hope you will feel confident in working through the material in this book. However, at some points in the series, you may want to call in a specialist—a Christian doctor, psychologist, nurse, or teacher—someone who has integrity and wisdom, and can put the kids at ease.

I would caution you about self-disclosure. You may have had difficulty with areas of your own sexuality in the past. Be sensitive about what you share concerning your own experiences. If not handled correctly, your group members may turn you off, look down on you, or convince themselves that because you did something, *they* have a right to do the same thing.

The Big Picture

Our desire for sex is God's idea. He thought it up. He did the plumbing. I used to think God made everything and then went on a coffee break, while Satan snuck in and gave us our sex organs. Sex is not evil or dirty—but it is powerful. Sex is like water or fire. On a hot day a cup of cold water can be refreshing. But water out of control, when a dam breaks, can destroy a town. On a cold night, a warm fire can feel very good. But fire out of control can destroy a home. Sex is wonderful within the framework it was intended. God created sex to be used and enjoyed. But, He created it to be used *within marriage* as an expression of total commitment and unity. Out of control, it can destroy a reputation and a life.

There are stronger desires than sex. For example, the desires for air and food are stronger. If you don't eat for seventy-one days, you won't be thinking about sex. You won't be thinking about anything. You'll be dead.

We have put sex on a pedestal in our society. Sex by itself will not bring happiness. If intercourse were the ultimate expression of love, then the happiest people on earth would be prostitutes. Instead those sad people find it almost impossible to love or be loved. Love is the warmth and acceptance communicated and demonstrated in hugs, glances, and the quiet moments of just holding each other.

"Going all the way" isn't fifteen minutes of ecstasy in the back seat of a car or a bedroom. It's two old people who have been married for forty-one years walking hand in hand around the park talking quietly to each other. Two friends and lovers. Any love that lasts that long is "going all the way."

Hugh Hefner, who bragged about going to bed with hundreds of women, got married a couple of years ago. When surprised reporters asked him why, he responded, "Because I'm lonely."

The Bible clearly states in I Thessalonians 4:3, "You should avoid sexual immorality." First Corinthians 6:18 instructs, "Flee from sexual immorality." I've heard kids say, "My body is my business." If you're a Christian, your body is the Lord's. The sad fact is that some kids' hearts are *not* broken by breaking the heart of God. God gives us His loving counsel on sex to make us *more* sexual, not less. God wants to teach us how to really love.

Consider Joseph, who was tempted by Potiphar's wife. He fled from her wearing only his jockey shorts. He didn't say "no" because he might get caught. He didn't say "no" because she might get pregnant. He didn't say "no" because he might get a sexually transmitted disease. He said "no" because it was a sin against God. "How then could I do such a wicked thing and sin against God?" he asked (Genesis 39:9). Imagine if your group members assumed a similar attitude.

May God bless and guide you as you embark on the journey of educating your group members concerning one of His most mysterious and precious gifts—sexuality.

Les Christie is a twenty-six-year veteran of youth ministry. He has been at the same church for twenty-one years. Les is a sought-after, popular national convention speaker to both youth and adults. He has authored dozens of articles and books, including Unsung Heroes *(Youth Specialties). He is married, has two children, and lives in Placentia, California.*

The images on these two pages are designed to help you promote this course within your church and community. Feel free to photocopy anything here and adapt it to fit your publicity needs. The stuff on this page could be used as a flier that you send or hand out to kids—or as a bulletin insert. The stuff on the next page could be used to add visual interest to newsletters, calendars, bulletin boards, or other promotions. Be creative and have fun!

Ever Had Thoughts about Sex?

If not, you can stay home. But if you have, join us as we start a new course called *Hormone Helper.*

Who:

When:

Where:

Questions? Call:

Hormone Helper

Hormone Helper

"Two thumbs up!!"
-Sickle and Eggbert

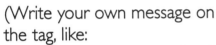

(Write your own message on the tag, like:
"Do not open until marriage"
or "To: [name of your group]
From: God")

The "S" word.

Questions about sex?

1 The Keys and the Car, but No License to Drive

YOUR GOALS FOR THIS SESSION:

Choose one or more

☐ To help kids become comfortable with the fact that they might be experiencing sexual feelings.

☐ (2) To help kids understand that while sex is a wonderful gift from God, it is incomplete (and inappropriate) outside the bond of marriage.

☐ (1) To help kids determine which physical aspects of sex are appropriate for this stage of their lives and commit to remain within those limitations.

☐ Other _____

_____

Your Bible Base:

Genesis 38
Ephesians 5:1-14
I Thessalonians 4:1-12

Sexual Scavenger Hunt

(Needed: Recent popular magazines, TV Guides, newspapers)

Form three or four teams, and give each team an equal number of magazines and newspapers. If possible, include a *TV Guide* for each team. Set a time limit (five to ten minutes), and announce that teams will be competing in a sexual scavenger hunt. Their goal will be to list the most references to sex (either overt or suggestive) from these sources:

• The newspapers you have provided (editorials, articles, comics, and so forth)

• The magazines you have provided (ads, articles, opinion columns, etc.)

• Listings in the *TV Guides*

• Any examples from recent TV programs that team members can recall

• Any examples from films or videos that team members have seen

• Any examples from song lyrics that team members can quote.

At the end of your predetermined time limit, have teams read their lists. The lists should be somewhat lengthy because any single source might provide numerous sexual references. The purpose of this exercise is to demonstrate the amount of sexual material that your young people are exposed to on a regular basis. As each list is read, the response from others is likely to be, "Oh, I didn't even think of that one."

Acknowledge the team that came up with the longest list. Then have group members quickly go back through their lists and identify any examples that they feel are pure or biblical examples of sexuality as opposed to those that contradict biblical standards. Have them figure a percentage of *positive* references based on the total.

Ask: **To what extent are you affected by the sexual messages you receive through the media?** If the tendency is to say, "Not at all," or "Very little," point out how many anti-Christian messages they were able to list at a moment's notice. Repetition is the key to any system of brainwashing, and the repeated references to more and better sex are certainly influential on young people. Your group members may be successfully repelling the messages—so far—yet it must certainly be a struggle for some of them to do so.

In what specific ways are you affected by all of these sexual messages? (Do sexy models in ads influence purchases of cologne, clothing, etc.? When the discussion turns to sex, do any of your group members feel inferior or left out? Does anyone act as if he or she is more experienced than he or she truly is, just to fit in?)

Why do you think so many people are uncomfortable talking about sex, even to the point of referring to it as "the birds and the bees," "doing the wild thing," and other such phrases? (Lack of adequate knowledge about the subject; embarrassment; to make it seem more commonplace and less special.)

Where do you get information that you trust about sex?

STEP
2

Is That in the Bible?

(Needed: Copies of Repro Resource 1, pens)

It is hoped that group members have a good understanding of what the Bible has to say about sexual purity. But some may be living under the assumption that the Bible is a bit behind the times when it comes to "current" issues such as romance and sexual activity. Hand out copies of "Is *That* in the Bible?" (Repro Resource 1). Have group members complete the quiz. When they're finished, discuss their answers. The correct responses are:

   (1) B [Proverbs 30:18, 19, New International Version]
   (2) B [Proverbs 11:22, Living Bible]
   (3) L [D. H. Lawrence]
   (4) F
   (5) B [Ecclesiastes 4:11, Living Bible]
   (6) B [Song of Songs 1:2, Living Bible]
   (7) B [Song of Songs 3:1, New International Version]
   (8) L [Francis Edward Smedley]
   (9) B [Song of Songs 7:1-3, Living Bible]
   (10) B [I Corinthians 7:3-5, Living Bible]
   (11) L [Emily Dickinson]
   (12) B [Song of Songs 7:7-9, Living Bible]
   (13) L [James Thurber]
   (14) B [I Corinthians 7:9, Living Bible]
   (15) F [Though the first sentence is quoted from Genesis 2:25, Living Bible]
   [Note: No quotations were taken from Dr. Ruth. Were any of your group members fooled?]
   Point out that God created sex to be one of the most pleasurable

experiences people can ever have. Sex is intended to be a wonderful gift. But like any gift of God, it can be misused and corrupted. Sex outside the bond of marriage causes a number of problems. And while these sessions will focus on several of those problems, we should never forget that sex was created as a unique, thrilling gift to bring two married people as close together as they can possibly be.

STEP 3

Caught after the Act

(Needed: Bibles, pens, paper)

O P T I O N S

Say: **You may discover that the Bible has a lot to say about sex that you don't know about. One story you probably never heard as a kid is found in Genesis 38. It's a bit complicated, but then so are most relationships where sexual activity is involved. It begins with Judah, who was one of the twelve sons of Jacob** (Israel). **He had three sons of his own— Er, Onan, and Shelah. When Er got old enough, Judah arranged for him to marry a girl named Tamar. But Er was not a good person, and God allowed him to die. According to the custom of the time, it then became the responsibility of the husband's brother to provide for the wife. And one of the means of "providing" was to marry her so she could bear children who would look after her** (Deuteronomy 25:5, 6). **This became the duty of Onan.**

However, Onan knew that an heir by Tamar could claim a significant portion of his inheritance. So he was willing to have sex with Tamar, but not to get her pregnant and give her a child. Consequently, he died also. With two sons down and only one to go, Judah got nervous.

Direct group members to Genesis 38. Have them read the chapter independently (or in small groups if they would be comfortable doing so). As they do, ask them to compile a list of "current" sexual issues they find—things that many young people are dealing with. Their discoveries should include

• using a partner for sexual fulfillment with no true commitment (vss. 9, 10)

• use of sex as a technique to manipulate someone else

• double standards (Judah was just as guilty as Tamar, but he was ready to kill *her*.)
• multiple sexual partners
• seduction (vs. 14)
• incest (vs. 16)
• potential scandal (vs. 24)
• birth control (vs. 9)
• prostitution
• rumor and accusation (vs. 24)
• blackmail (vs. 25)

Explain that in this case, the problems were resolved. Judah was caught after the act—red faced, no doubt—and took responsibility for his actions. Tamar got the child(ren) she wanted, even though her method was by no means honorable. And one of the babies born from the sexual liaison between Judah and Tamar was Perez, an ancestor of King David (Ruth 4:18-22), and subsequently, of Jesus. So God can create good things, even from the mistakes we make.

Summarize: **The Bible contains many similar stories of the unfortunate and often tragic consequences of sexual misconduct: homosexual acts, incest, abuse, rape, and so forth. However, it also tells us how we can avoid the potential pitfalls of getting involved in a relationship built entirely on sexual drive rather than genuine love.**

STEP 4

Sex: Now and Then

(Needed: Note paper, pens, fake microphone)

Spend a little time explaining how our society's thinking has evolved in regard to marriage (and consequently, "permissible" sex). Explain that in Bible times, marriages took place much sooner after puberty. As soon as someone was able to *become* a parent, he or she had the *opportunity* to do so as well. The person simply got married and started a family. But our current society has come up with the concept of *adolescence*, a period during which time teenagers have the sexual capacities of an adult, but are expected to wait for several years until they are "mature" enough to get married.

See if you can find one or two volunteers who will speak out in favor of marriage (and "legitimate" sex) at this point in their lives, and a

couple of others willing to cope with not acting on their hormonal urges for several more years until they do get married. (Explain that these are the only two biblically acceptable options for young people wishing to become sexually active.) Call these volunteers to the front as you play the role of a talk show host. Wander through the group with a fake microphone, letting members ask questions or make comments, and try to generate a good discussion. Keep the conversation balanced, alternating between the pros and cons of either side. Questions to consider might include:

• **Do you think it's fair to be expected to wait several years before acting on sexual urges you may already feel? Why or why not?**

• **If you could get married as soon as you began to get sexual urges, how do you think it would affect your lifestyle? Your behavior? Your other relationships (parents, friends, etc.)?**

• **What would you think about having your parents arrange a marriage for you, as parents frequently did in ancient cultures?**

• **Would you rather be treated as an adult right now—with all the responsibilities of finding a job, providing for a family, etc.—or would you prefer having a few more years of "carefree" adolescence, even though you may still be treated as a child by parents, teachers, and so forth?**

After the discussion, summarize: **Regardless of your opinion, the fact is that in our society most of you are expected to wait for a number of years before you get married. In the meantime, you are likely to have some strong sexual urges.**

 What reasons do young people give to justify having sex before they get married? (They love each other; everyone else is doing it; they plan to marry the other person eventually; sex is no big deal anymore; sex is a "rite of passage" into adulthood; etc.)

 What do you say in response to your friends who have these opinions? Let group members comment, but let them know that you will be providing them with some good answers in this and subsequent sessions.

Group members may fully believe that God has condemned premarital sex, but not know exactly where to find proof. The seventh commandment, "You shall not commit adultery" (Exodus 20:14), doesn't say anything about *premarital* sex.

Divide into groups. Have each group read one of the two following passages and create a list of things people need to keep in mind as they deal with sex on a physical basis—guidelines, warnings, challenges, etc. (Suggested responses are provided.) One person from each group should report his or her group's answers to the whole group.

Ephesians 5:1-14

• We should imitate God (in purity, holiness, etc.).

• Our actions should not even *hint* of sexual immorality.

• Dirty jokes and obscene language should be avoided.

• We shouldn't be fooled by people who try to deceive us into believing lies.

• What people do in secret will be exposed.

I Thessalonians 4:1-12

• We should live to please God (rather than ourselves).

• God's people are to be "sanctified" (distinctive as compared to the rest of the sinful world).

• We should learn to control our bodies and avoid sexual immorality.

• Sex should not be considered an option, because it takes advantage of someone else.

• God will punish sexual immorality.

• We should be more concerned with earning others' respect than keeping up with them sexually.

STEP
5

A Hands-Off Approach

(Needed: Copies of Repro Resource 2, pens)

Astute group members may have noted by this time that not *all* physical aspects of sex are necessarily wrong. If not, challenge the assumption that being "sexual" means having intercourse. Ask: **Are there appropriate ways for someone your age to express physical attraction toward someone of the opposite sex? If so, what are they?** List responses. In some cases, there may be disagreement as to the appropriateness of certain actions. If so, save discussion for later. You're simply making a list of responses right now.

Hand out copies of "Let's Get Physical" (Repro Resource 2), which lists several types of physical expression. Let group members add anything they came up with that isn't already listed. Then have them place each activity at the point on the scale where they feel it belongs. (As they do, be sure to have them consult the lists of biblical guidelines they compiled earlier.) For example, one person might be a "hugger" who in all innocence enjoys the warm and fuzzy feeling a hug brings. To someone else, however, it might invoke lustful thoughts and lead to temptation. So while the first person would find hugging "Perfectly Acceptable," the other person might need to list as "Potentially Dangerous."

O P T I O N S

LARGE GROUP

MOSTLY GIRLS

JR.HIGH
HIGH SCHOOL
COMBINED

When group members finish, let willing volunteers compare their sheets and see if there are any significant differences. As members discover what behaviors others feel are appropriate, they may become more comfortable as they relate to each other.

Challenge each person to learn to enjoy the sexual physical sensations that are appropriate for him or her at this time, and to avoid going farther and getting more involved than he or she intends to.

Summarize: **It may seem to you that the sexual feelings you have are something like being given a brand new Porsche, having the keys in your hand, and knowing everything you think you need to know about driving—yet being several years away from being able to get a driver's license. As tempting as it might be to go ahead and take all the risks involved with breaking the law, if you do, you're almost certain to face severe consequences somewhere down the line.**

Worth the Wait? (Part I)

(Needed: Paper, pens)

Each of these sessions will conclude with three specific reasons why it is worth saving sexual intercourse for marriage. Group members should be encouraged to add other reasons of their own. Essentially, the only reasons young people give for having premarital sex are: (1) to "prove" love; (2) because they just couldn't stop when they got involved; or (3) because it's "no big deal." All of these "justifications" will be refuted. But in the meantime, the list of reasons to save sex for marriage should be significantly longer and should make a lot of sense. (And if group members come up with the reasons themselves, they might be more willing to follow their own advice.)

Begin by thinking only of the *physical* reasons to save sex for marriage. A few of the things your young people should come up with are listed below.

When you save sex for marriage:

• All risk of premarital pregnancy (and its many complications) is eliminated.

• The risk of contracting the sexually transmitted HIV (AIDS) virus is greatly reduced.

• The risk of contracting other sexually transmitted diseases (syphilis, gonorrhea, etc.) disappears.

If these were the only three reasons to put off having sex, they should be plenty, but there are many more to come. Birth control pills, condoms, and other paraphernalia may reduce such risks, but can never entirely prevent them. Faithfulness within a monogamous marriage relationship is the only genuine "safe" sex.

Keep in mind that many times the sex drive is strong enough to overrule logic. As you close in prayer, ask God to provide your group members with the physical willpower and emotional integrity they need to remain sexually pure in an age of promiscuous activity. And if you plan to go on with this series, tell them that the emotional aspects of sex may be even more significant than the physical ones—as they'll find out next time.

Is That in the
BIBLE?

Read each of the following quotations. If you think it comes from the Bible, place a "B" beside the quote. If you think it comes from a famous literary writer, mark it with an "L." If you think it comes from Dr. Ruth, use a "D." And if you think we just made it up, give it an "F" (for "fictional"). Be warned, however, that we used the Living Bible for some of the biblical quotes so you wouldn't get any clues from the "thees" and "thous."

_____ 1. "There are three things that are too amazing for me, four that I do not understand: the way of an eagle in the sky, the way of a snake on a rock, the way of a ship on the high seas, and the way of a man with a maiden."

_____ 2. "A beautiful woman lacking discretion and modesty is like a fine gold ring in a pig's snout."

_____ 3. "Sex and beauty are inseparable, like life and consciousness. And the intelligence which goes with sex and beauty, and arises out of sex and beauty, is intuition."

_____ 4. "God has a specific person selected for you, and when the time is right, you will know His will in the matter."

_____ 5. "On a cold night, two under the same blanket gain warmth from each other, but how can one be warm alone?"

_____ 6. "Kiss me again and again, for your love is sweeter than wine."

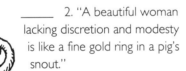

_____ 7. "All night long on my bed I looked for the one my heart loves; I looked for him but did not find him."

_____ 8. "All's fair in love and war."

_____ 9. "How beautiful your tripping feet, O queenly maiden. Your rounded thighs are like jewels....Your navel is lovely as a goblet filled with wine. Your waist is like a heap of wheat set about with lilies. Your two breasts are like two fawns, yes, lovely twins."

_____ 10. "The man should give his wife all that is her right as a married woman, and the wife should do the same for her husband: for a girl who marries no longer has full right to her own body, for her husband then has his rights to it, too; and in the same way the husband no longer has full right to his own body, for it belongs also to his wife. So do not refuse these rights to each other."

_____ 11. "That Love is all there is, is all we know of Love."

_____ 12. "You are tall and slim like a palm tree, and your breasts are like its clusters of dates. I said, I will climb up into the palm tree and take hold of its branches. Now may your breasts be like grape clusters, and the scent of your breath like apples, and your kisses as exciting as the best of wine, smooth and sweet, causing the lips of those who are asleep to speak."

_____ 13. "I love the idea of there being two sexes, don't you?"

_____ 14. "It is better to marry than to burn with lust."

_____ 15. "Now although the man and his wife were both naked, neither of them was embarrassed or ashamed. And God said, 'You two try to control yourselves, OK?'"

Let's Get Physical

Sex has a lot of different physical aspects. One is intercourse, which you are told is wrong before marriage. Another is holding hands, which even your parents will admit is "Oh, how cute!" And in between the two is a whole range of other possibilities. Some of these may be things that seem acceptable for other people, yet which make you uncomfortable. So this scale is for you. Go through the list of physical sensations and place the number of each one in the box where you feel it belongs.

1. Holding hands on a moonlit night

2. Slow dancing

3. "Full contact" dancing

4. Going "all the way"

5. A goodnight peck on the cheek

6. Hugging

7. Giving a back rub

8. Getting a back rub

9. A heavy "back seat" make-out session

10. Mutual fondling to the point of arousal

11. Oral sex

12. Playing "Post Office," "Spin the Bottle," etc.

13. Calling "900" numbers for sexual conversations

14. Full body massage

15. Passionate kissing

CLEARLY WRONG

POTENTIALLY DANGEROUS

PERFECTLY ACCEPTABLE

Step 1

If cutting up magazines wouldn't be active enough for your group, try this variation. Before the session, cut at least a dozen photos of "beautiful people" (plus a few ordinary ones) from magazines. To start your meeting, give each person one or more pictures. When you give the signal, kids have to arrange the faces in a line on the floor in order of "sexiness" from left to right, least to most. When there's a disagreement over the place a picture should have, majority rules. Then discuss the fact that sexiness is in the eye of the beholder. Ask: **Why do we think some people are sexy and others aren't? If sex is a personal, private thing, why do many people try so hard to look sexy? How do you think God feels about the question of what's sexy and what isn't?**

Step 3

Instead of studying Genesis 38, read Genesis 1:26-28; 2:18-25 aloud. Have kids run up to the board and draw the "male" symbol (a circle connected to an arrow) whenever a male is mentioned, and a "female" sign (a circle connected to a cross) whenever a female is mentioned—and a heart shape whenever something is mentioned involving the two of them. Ask: **What can we learn from these verses about sex and God's attitude toward it?** (Possible answers: God created the sexes; He declared them [including their bodies] good; the male and female needed each other; God expected them to have sex [as part of multiplying and in order to be one flesh]; the man and woman were meant to have no shame about their bodies or their sexuality.)

Step 1

When discussing a sensitive subject like sexuality, there can be safety in numbers; kids who are embarrassed can hope that someone else will answer your questions. But if you're one of just two or three kids, there's nowhere to hide. Unless your kids are especially comfortable with each other, don't expect them to warm up easily to discussion. Arrange seating as informally as you can, with seats at a 45-degree angle to each other rather than making kids face each other head-on. Ask potentially embarrassing questions in the third person instead of first person. Give kids time to think about questions that they don't feel comfortable answering aloud. In Step 1, if your group is too small to make the scavenger hunt a team effort, let kids compete individually.

Step 4

If you have fewer than eight group members, it may be tough to make the talk-show format work. Try substituting a radio call-in format so that panelists won't be needed. Bring a disconnected phone receiver. Act as the host, throwing out questions for "callers" to answer. Give the phone to a group member, then ask the first question. He or she answers, then gives the phone to someone else. If you like, announce that you'll ask a question of "the fifteenth caller," and have kids pass the phone around that many times before asking the next question.

Step 3

If your group is large enough, provide added incentive for reading Genesis 38 by dividing the group into five teams: lawyers for Tamar, lawyers for Judah, prosecutors who have charged Tamar with prostitution and blackmail, prosecutors who have charged Judah with buying the services of a prostitute, and members of the Society for More Decent Bibles, who believe all references to sex should be removed from Scripture. After giving teams time to read the chapter, the lawyers and prosecutors should make their cases to the rest of the group. Then have the members of the Society for More Decent Bibles tell how they'd like to censor the chapter—allowing you to lead into a discussion of how Scripture frankly treats the subject of sex.

Step 5

Sharing and comparing kids' responses to Repro Resource 2 may be difficult to do thoroughly in a large group. To expedite the process, divide your meeting place into three zones: Clearly Wrong, Potentially Dangerous, and Perfectly Acceptable. As you read the items on the list, give kids time to arrange themselves in the three zones to show how they responded. Let volunteers explain their answers before moving from one item to the next.

HEARD IT ALL BEFORE

LITTLE BIBLE BACKGROUND

FELLOWSHIP & WORSHIP

Step 4
Kids who have spent much time in church won't be surprised to hear that the Bible opposes sexual immorality. They may question the relevance of such an old book to the urgent drives they feel. So ease into discussion of biblical morality with the following simulation. Say: **The year is 2418. You have just been appointed commander of a space station orbiting the planet Gamma IV in the Andromeda galaxy. You have inherited all kinds of problems from the last commander. Sexually transmitted diseases are running rampant throughout the station, killing several key personnel each year; 25% of your unmarried teenage girls are having babies, placing an added burden on your life support system; several rapes are reported each week. Yet none of these problems exist on Gamma IV, where an alien civilization lives by a strict rule: no sexual relations outside of marriage. Your space station has no rules governing sexual behavior, but offers free condoms, free abortions, and free meetings with android prostitutes. What do you do about your problems, and why?**

Step 6
Jaded kids might rattle off the right "why wait" answers, knowing what's expected. But the answers may have no connection to their behavior. Instead of asking such kids to list physical reasons why *they* should abstain from premarital sex, ask what they would tell younger brothers or sisters to do. Then ask whether the same advice should apply to themselves, and why.

Step 3
Given the complexity of Genesis 38, you may be better off reading Genesis 1:26-28; 2:18-25 (see "Extra Action" option). If you want to use Genesis 38, you'll need to explain three things:
• Some of ancient Israel's customs (such as taking the wife of a deceased brother) differed from those we should follow today. In some cases God gave commands that fit Israel's situation and not ours, and in some cases Moses allowed less-than-perfect practices because people resisted following God's way (as with divorce; see Matthew 19:7-9).
• People in Bible times felt a stronger need to have large families than many people in our culture feel today. Children were needed as helpers in an agricultural society, and the death rate for babies was high. This helps to explain, though not excuse, Tamar's behavior.
• The Bible reports all kinds of behavior, good and bad. It doesn't always go into detail about the wrongness of all the sins it reports. We shouldn't assume that just because something's mentioned here that it's okay.

Step 4
Before asking kids to analyze the Ephesians and I Thessalonians passages, you may want to explain that the Greek word translated "sexual immorality" here is *porneia*. It refers to a wide range of sexual activities condemned by God—such as adultery, intercourse before and outside of marriage, prostitution, incest, and other perversions or distortions of the way God meant sex to be. Kids may think these verses fail to specifically prohibit premarital sex, but the fact is that they condemn premarital sex and much more.

Step 1
Kids may feel nervous and a little embarrassed when they hear sexuality is the subject of this session. Acknowledge those feelings while helping kids get to know each other with the following activity. Form pairs, mixing guys and girls as much as possible. Give each pair a small amount of "blusher" makeup and a brush, sponge, or cotton ball with which to apply it. (If some girls in your group have makeup in their purses, let them use it.) One person in each pair should brush a little blusher on his or her partner's cheeks while the one receiving the blush describes an "embarrassing moment" he or she has experienced. Then have the partners switch roles. When everyone is "blushing," note that it sometimes feels embarrassing to talk about sex—but that you won't be putting anybody on the spot in this meeting. Be sure to provide plenty of makeup remover for kids to use as you move into the rest of the session.

Step 6
To conclude, ask kids to close their eyes and to imagine that they've traveled back in time to the creation of the world. They're watching God at work in the Garden of Eden. Read or have a volunteer read Genesis 1:26-28, 31 and Psalm 139:13-16. Then, with kids' eyes still closed, say something like this: **God invented sex. He also invented you, every bit of you, including your sexuality. You may not always feel like a great invention, but you are. Take a minute now to tell God how you feel about being a guy or a girl and to thank Him for inventing sex and inventing you.** Then close in prayer yourself, thanking God for the kids in your group and the way He's created them.

MOSTLY GIRLS

Step 1

After discussing sexual messages and influences, distribute paper and pencils and ask the girls to write the names of the adults in their immediate world (parents, teachers, church leaders). Have them mark the ones they think are appropriate models of biblical standards for human sexuality. Then ask the girls to use one corner of their paper to write their responses to the following questions. **Do you think you know everything you need to know about how your body functions? About a guy's body? Who are the people on your list you can talk to for more information?**

Step 5

After discussing Repro Resource 2, have the girls talk about the items on the sheet that may be acceptable but could become potentially dangerous. Form teams of three or four girls and give each team a different item. Ask each team to suggest a few things that might be done if an acceptable situation begins to change. For example, what if a back rub isn't limited to your back, or a friendly hug becomes more. Ask: **What can you do or say? What if the guy is someone you admire and whose friendship you don't want to lose?**

MOSTLY GUYS

Step 4

If your group is mainly male, or if you're splitting the group along gender lines for these sessions, you may want to focus on issues many guys face. Have one team read the Ephesians verses and discuss: **Does a hint of sexual immorality** (vs. 3) **make a guy more attractive to girls? Does it make him feel better about himself? Does a hint of sexual immorality make a girl more or less attractive? Why? Do you agree that dirty jokes** (vs. 4) **are always out of place? Why or why not? Which do you think is more attractive to most guys: dirty jokes or giving thanks? How does one tend to prevent the other?** Have another team read the I Thessalonians passage and discuss: **How could a guy tell that he hadn't learned to control his own body** (vs. 4)**? What are some places you might avoid if you were trying to learn to control your sexual appetite? How might a Christian guy wrong another Christian sexually** (vs. 6)**? How could brotherly (or sisterly) love** (vs. 9) **prevent that?**

Step 6

For many adolescent males, the sex drive is so strong that abstinence sounds like a guarantee of physical suffering. They lose sight of the fact that sex is not a life-or-death physical need like breathing, eating, and drinking. Give them a visual reminder of this fact by taping on the wall the following pictures you've drawn or photocopied and labeled beforehand: a human skull labeled "Three hours without breathing"; a human skull labeled "Three months without food"; a human skull labeled "Three months without water"; and a smiling, healthy guy labeled "Three years without sex."

EXTRA FUN

Step 1

Stage a two-team relay race. Kids from one team (The Pleasure Seekers) try to make it across the room to pick up cookies one at a time and bring them back. Kids from the other team (The Pleasure Police) try to keep the Pleasure Seekers from accomplishing their goal. If a police officer tags a cookie smuggler, the latter has to put the cookie back. The Pleasure Seekers have three minutes (or another time limit that fits the size of your group) to get all the cookies. If they succeed, they keep the cookies. If not, the cookies go to the Pleasure Police. After the contest, lead into the question of whether God is like the Pleasure Police—trying to keep people from enjoying their natural sexuality.

Step 6

After the meeting, set up a refreshment table. At first put "Hands Off!" and "Do Not Touch!" signs on everything kids might like. Then take those signs off and put up signs that limit the amount each person can take, plus some that indicate in what order kids can eat the items. Point out that God's approach is to give us limits for our own good, not to deny us what is good.

Step 1

During the week before the meeting, use a VCR to tape a TV program like *Entertainment Tonight* or a music video show. Include the commercials. To start your meeting, play the program for your group—but in the fast-forward or "search" mode, so that kids can see the show in fast motion. (Note: so that images don't flash by too quickly to see, tape the program on your VCR's "SP" speed.) Encourage kids to mentally keep track of the number of images they see that seem to be using sex or sexiness to get attention. After watching for about five minutes, see who came up with the most and least images and why. Then pick up the basic session's Step 1 with the question: **To what extent are you affected by the sexual messages you receive through the media?**

Step 4

Rather than using the talk-show format, play a song for the group: the Beach Boys' "Wouldn't It Be Nice." This oldie sounds downright quaint today, expressing a boy's yearning for the intimacy he'd have with his girlfriend if they were only older and married. If you have time, play a current song that takes for granted a sexual relationship without any reference to commitment. Contrast the two songs. Whether playing one song or both, ask: **What percentage of dating teenagers today do you think have the attitude of the singer in "Wouldn't It Be Nice"? Why does this song sound old-fashioned today?** Then use the talk-show questions in the basic session's Step 4.

Step 1

Combine Steps 1 and 2 into a single opener. Before the meeting, cut a variety of ads, especially movie and clothing ads, from magazines; cut the quotes from Repro Resource 1, separating each quote from the rest. Put all of these items in a pile in the middle of your meeting place. As your session begins, designate one wall "Goes Along with the Bible" and another "Doesn't Go Along with the Bible." Kids should line up at the pile, each taking one ad or quote and taping it on one wall or the other without comment. Then let the whole group look at the two walls and discuss whether they agree or disagree with the way the quotes and ads were categorized.

Step 3

Skip the study of Genesis 38 and return to the nine biblical quotes on Repro Resource 1. Have kids cross out the six that aren't from the Bible, and discuss the way love and sex are viewed in these quotes. Note that sex and love are tied together, that sex is seen in a mostly positive light, and that sexuality is treated frankly. Are group members surprised by this? What has been their impression of the Bible's view of sex until now? Then read Step 4's Ephesians *or* I Thessalonians passage. After pulling out the main points, move back to the middle of Step 4 and ask the whole group just one or two of the "talk-show" questions. If time is very limited, skip Steps 5 and 6. In their place, pass out photocopies of a portion of Les Christie's article, "Talking to Kids about Sex," from the beginning of this book. The portion you should photocopy begins with the subhead, "The Big Picture," and finishes three paragraphs from the end of the article, with the sentence, "God wants to teach us how to really love." Let kids take this home to read.

Step 1

Instead of using magazines, do this activity with music CDs or albums. The objective is to write down as many sexual inferences as can be found in the albums before the time is up. Have your teens bring CDs or albums of their favorite R & B and rap artists. The activity will work best if you have a wide range of contemporary artists (Public Enemy, 2 Live Crew, Shabba Ranks, MC Hammer, Whitney Houston, BBD, Mariah Carey, etc.). Display the CDs or albums exhibition style on tables around the room. Then give your group members a time limit for the activity. When you say go, they will move around the room, writing down the sexual inferences they find on the CDs or albums.

Step 4

The talk-show format can have a further impact by including teenagers (male and female) who already have children. To a number of urban churches and youth groups this is an accessible reality. Interestingly, these young people tend to preach a "gospel of sexual responsibility" after having a child. They want to share with their peers the lessons they did not heed concerning sexual responsibility. They will probably share in direct and straightforward language that marriage and/or sexual responsibility ought to be considered. This type of peer counseling will cause good and frank discussion among teens, and will get them beyond the intimidation of asking the youth worker sexual questions in a public format.

Step I

If possible, separate junior high and high school students while leading these sessions. If you can't, remember that some junior highers are in the confusion of mid-puberty, while older kids may be battling (or succumbing to) temptation. Assume that all the kids are curious about sex and that some may be experienced, but don't assume that all kids are dating or that all understand the biological basics. Keep discussion in the third person as much as possible to avoid putting younger kids on the spot (Example: Instead of asking, **Where do you get information about sex?** ask, **Where do the kids you know get information about sex?** Give kids from both age groups a nonthreatening way to ask specific questions by using a question box (a shoebox with a slot in the top), into which kids can drop written queries for you to answer. For Step 3, use the "Extra Action" option (reading Genesis 1:26-28; 2:18-25 instead of Genesis 38). In Step 4, don't expect younger kids to have answers to the questions asked by the "talk-show host"; you may want to address these to older kids. In the same step, use either the Ephesians *or* the I Thessalonians passage, not both, and try to include a mix of ages in each small group so that older kids can help younger ones.

Step 5

Kids who have struggled with the "How far can I go?" question may find Repro Resource 2 helpful. But some younger students may find it confusing and a little scary—and their parents may fear that explicit discussion of petting will "put ideas in" kids' minds. If you think the latter is the case in your group, delete the sheet and discuss ways in which kids have seen people on TV and in movies express affection. Which would they be comfortable with? Which ways do they think are OK? Which aren't?

Step I

If cutting up magazines would seem too much like a grade-school craft project to your young people, open with a slightly more cerebral activity. Pass out paper and pens. Each person must write a one-hundred-word description of a typical day in his or her life—without using the letters S, E, or X. Allow up to five minutes for kids to meet this challenge; if you like, give a prize to anyone who is successful. After noting the difficulty of the assignment, tie it into the challenge of life without SEX—living without being sexually active, even though one has the physical ability to have sex.

Step 6

At the end of the session, form pairs. Offer a prize to any pairs who take on one of the following assignments this week: (1) Write a "book report" on the section of your school health textbook that deals with sexuality, and read it to the group next week; (2) prepare to debate each other for five minutes on the subject of whether school-based clinics should be allowed to distribute condoms; or (3) prepare (and perform next week) a skit in which characters from a show like *Melrose Place* or *Beverly Hills 90210* discover that they won't die if they don't have sex.

Date Used:

Approx.
Time

Step I: Sexual Scavenger Hunt _____
o Extra Action
o Small Group
o Fellowship & Worship
o Mostly Girls
o Extra Fun
o Media
o Short Meeting Time
o Urban
o Combined Junior High/High School
o Extra Challenge
Things needed:

Step 2: Is That ... _____
Things needed:

Step 3: Caught after ... _____
o Extra Action
o Large Group
o Little Bible Background
o Short Meeting Time
Things needed:

Step 4: Sex ... _____
o Small Group
o Heard It All Before
o Little Bible Background
o Mostly Guys
o Media
o Urban
Things needed:

Step 5: A Hands-Off ... _____
o Large Group
o Mostly Girls
o Combined Junior High/High School
Things needed:

Step 6: Worth the Wait ... _____
o Heard It All Before
o Fellowship & Worship
o Mostly Guys
o Extra Fun
o Extra Challenge
Things needed:

2 R-E-S-P-E-C-T: That's What Sex Should Mean to Thee

YOUR GOALS FOR THIS SESSION:

Choose one or more

☐ To help kids realize that sex is not the most natural or logical result of genuine love during a relationship prior to marriage.

☐ To help kids identify and deal with the many emotions that accompany sexual desire and/or activity.

☐ To help kids begin to associate the importance of respect with any type of sexual desire and/or opportunity.

☐ Other _____

Your Bible Base:

Genesis 34
Galatians 5:22, 23

STEP

1

Picture This Emotion

(Needed: Written-out sets of emotions, drawing paper, pens, "Love Indicator" circles)

Form teams and provide each team with a pen and plenty of paper. Have teams assemble in the corners of the room, as far from each other as possible. In the center of the room, provide for each team a set of folded slips of paper which contain a variety of emotions, behaviors, and feelings (joy, hatred, lust, hunger, grief, despair, disappointment, peace, kindness, loneliness, greed, and so forth). Each slip of paper should contain one emotion. An identical set of folded slips should be provided for each team. At your signal, one person from each team should run to his or her stack, draw one slip of paper, run back to his or her team members, and attempt to draw the word using *Pictionary* rules (no talking, no use of letters or numbers, etc.). After the word is guessed, the next person in the group should repeat the process. Team members should alternate until all the slips are gone or until you call time. The first team to draw and guess all the words successfully, or that completes the most within your time limit, is the winner.

Explain that as young people begin to have sexual feelings and try to work through what they are experiencing, they go through a wide range of emotions. The emotions can vary from day to day. To find out what your group members are feeling *now*, convert your room into a "Love Indicator" machine—like one you might find at a carnival or arcade (the kind where the person puts in a quarter and a light bulb comes on to indicate how "sexy" he or she is). Put down circles or squares of paper across the room, with escalating levels such as "Ice Queen/King," "Cold Fish," "Cool and Clammy," "Meek and Mild," "Middle of the Road," "On the Spicy Side," "Hot Tamale," and "Volcano."

Let group members choose where they think they belong and stand on that spot. After all group members have taken a position, see if they agree with each other's self-assessments. Discuss: **How does it make you feel to be perceived as less romantic than you really are? How do you feel to be thought of as "sexier" than you think you are?**

A Skit and It Shall Be Done for You

Ask for volunteers to perform some skits. Volunteers should act out one or more of the following scenes and focus on the *feelings* of the person(s) involved. Read each scenario and give volunteers a few minutes to put something together.

(1) Andrew has never had a date, though most of his friends have been dating for a number of years. But out of the blue, Angie asks him to a turnabout event at school. They have a wonderful time, and Andrew suddenly realizes the thrill of dating. Volunteers should put together a before-and-after skit to contrast Andrew's emotional state prior to the party with how he acts the day after.

(2) Jane has begun to date Ted. Jane has never dated much, but Ted has had several relationships—some of them involving considerable sexual activity. The guys in the locker room like to hear Ted talk about his dates and the things he has done. Jane and Ted haven't gotten involved more than an occasional good-night kiss. None of Ted's other girlfriends really meant that much to him, but he really likes Jane. The problem is that his friends press him for "the juicy details" in the locker room every Monday. Volunteers should enact the locker room as the guys try to get Ted to talk. Will he tell them the truth, or what they want to hear?

(3) Jeannie and Jason are the "perfect couple" at school. Both are smart and athletic, and have big plans for the future. They have dated for about three years, and are planning to attend the same college. However, on this particular day, Jeannie pulls Jason aside (some of their friends might be hanging around) to tell him that she is pregnant. Jason and Jeannie should express what they are feeling toward each other, and begin to explore their options.

(4) The biblical Mary confronts the biblical Joseph to tell him she is pregnant—and why. Mary and Joseph should express their feelings and explore their options as Jason and Jeannie did in the previous example.

Summarize: **Sex is certainly a physical act, and can have physical consequences—pregnancy, sexually transmitted diseases, etc. Yet perhaps even more powerful are the** emotions that accompany a sexual relationship. The emotions we feel during the early stages of love, or romance, at least, can be so incredibly thrilling that we never want them to end. We want more and more. But if we allow emotions to lead us to sexual activity, we suddenly find ourselves facing a whole load of other emotions. The physical thrill of sex is short-lived. The emotions are ongoing—almost continual. That's why God designed sex to take place only within the context of marriage. When two people are wholly and eternally committed to each other, sex brings them together and makes them feel wonderful. But outside of marriage, sex ignites the wrong emotions: fear, shame, jealousy, guilt, and more.

STEP

3

Hitting below the Belt

(Needed: Bibles, pens, paper)

O P T I O N S

Explain that many times the strong emotions that accompany pre-marital sex aren't limited to the two people who become sexually active. Many others may be involved as well—parents, friends, children who might result from such a union, etc.

For a case in point, divide into groups, hand out paper and pens, and have group members read Genesis 34. This chapter provides the account of Shechem's rape of Dinah (the daughter of Jacob). As group members read through the chapter, have them list all the emotions they discover, either stated or implied. Also ask them to put themselves into the roles of the characters in the account and list the emotions they think they would be feeling. They should put together a long list, including:

• Betrayal (vs. 1—Dinah had been to visit the women of the land, strangers to her)
• Lust (vs. 2)
• "Love" (vs. 3)
• Passion/desire (vs. 4)
• "Grief and fury" (vs. 7)
• Disgrace/shame (vs. 7)
• Deceit (vss. 13-17)
• Delight (vs. 19)

- Greed (vss. 20-23)
- Revenge (vss. 25, 26)
- Retribution (vss. 27-29)
- Fear (vs. 30)
- Honor (vs. 31)

Ask: **How did Dinah feel about what had happened?** (We don't know. Of all the emotions listed in this chapter, we are unable to determine how *she* felt. Was she glad that her brothers had wiped out the family of Shechem? Or would she have liked to have married him, in spite of what he had done to her? Though she was the victim in this story, we know less of what *she* felt than of what all the others were feeling.)

Put yourself in Dinah's place. You can see, to some extent, the depth of emotions that resulted from one sexual encounter. Some of the people around you are excited. Others are violently angry. And most of them are confused and acting in irrational ways. The same thing happens every time someone chooses to have sex prior to marriage. The person's life can never be the same, nor can the lives of his or her family members.

STEP

4

Name That Feeling

(Needed: Pens, paper, copies of Repro Resources 3 and 4)

Hand out pens and paper as you explain that you are going to read a number of statements kids might hear at school. After each statement, group members should immediately write the emotion(s) they would feel upon hearing that statement. When they're finished (give them just a few seconds), have group members simultaneously hold up what they have written. This should both encourage group members to be honest and allow them to see how often other people may feel the same way they do. It will also allow you to get some insight into how they truly feel as they deal with sexual issues at school. The following are some sample statements, but feel free to add others that you know would be specifically applicable to your group.

• A person you really like, but you don't think likes you, walks up and says, "I have two tickets to a concert this weekend. Would you like to go?"

• **A person you barely know, but find very annoying, walks up and says, "I have two tickets to a concert this weekend. Would you like to go?"**

✗ **Your best friend pulls you aside and tells you, "Chris and I went 'all the way' last night!"**

• **Your friend Gina has a boyfriend named Scott that you've never liked at all. Gina tells you, "Scott forced me to have sex with him last night. I kept saying no, but he just wouldn't stop."**

• **One of your biggest adversaries walks up to you in front of a crowd of people and says, quite loudly, "Is it true what I hear? Are you a *virgin*?!"**

• **A casual friend says, "You and a date are invited to a party at Bill's tonight. It's couples only, and his parents won't be home—if you know what I mean."**

In some cases, it may be difficult for group members to identify exactly what they would be feeling. Summarize: **As you can see, sexual activity can arouse a lot of strong emotions—even if you aren't the one involved in the sexual activity. The emotions range from sheer joy to horrifying terror. That's why it's so important to do everything in your power to avoid those strong, negative emotions.**

Distribute copies of "The Gift." Repro Resources 3 and 4 are designed to look alike, but there are subtle and significant differences. Half of your group members should get one version and the other half should get the other version. But all group members should assume they're getting the same assignment.

After group members read the parable, ask: **What do you think the "gift" represents?** (Sexual intercourse.)

Who do you think the giver is? (Though we may tend to think we give sex to someone we love, it is first and foremost a gift to each of us from God.)

Do you identify at all with the anticipation Joe felt?
Do you think Joe did the right thing?
Is Joe's model one that you would like to follow?
How do you think Joe felt at the end of the story?

Try to start with some questions that everyone will agree with, but eventually let group members discover that two versions of the story have been circulated. Explain that it's the same way in life—we all have pretty much the same opportunities, and it's how we respond to those opportunities that shapes our attitudes toward the people we date, the sexual act itself, and pretty much our whole state of mind.

STEP 5

The Logical Results

(Needed: Bibles)

It is likely that group members will agree with much of what you have said so far. Many of them probably have friends who have been hurt by getting too involved with sex too quickly. Yet most young people struggle with the "big" question, so let them deal with it now: **What if you really love the other person? Isn't sex a logical, natural, and justifiable way of deepening that love?** (A related question is "What if you have every intention to marry the other person? What's the big deal about getting started a little early with the sexual activity?")

Let group members discuss their opinions. Perhaps some of them have thought through the issue and have good answers. But for others, it might still be a struggle. When the discussion begins to wane a bit, have someone read aloud Galatians 5:22, 23. Then ask: **If we're living as the Christians God has created us to be, what will be the logical results of love?**

Let group members discover the characteristics associated with love in regard to the fruit of the Spirit. Ask: **Do you think these qualities really apply to romantic and sexual relationships?** (Yes. In the context of the chapter, they are contrasted with such things as "sexual immorality," "debauchery," and "orgies" [Galatians 5:19-22].)

One at a time, read the qualities associated with love in this passage (joy, peace, patience, kindness, goodness, faithfulness, gentleness, and self-control). In each case, determine whether the characteristic would be evident in most relationships where sexual activity is taking place. Then determine in what ways it might be apparent in relationships where both people have committed to refrain from sex. (For instance, patience would certainly be evident in a relationship in which two people are waiting until they're married to have sex.)

When you finish, summarize: **What all this boils down to is that sexual activity demonstrates a lack of respect for the other person. Genuine love promotes patience, self-control, and gentleness. Premarital sexual involvement is usually based on selfish needs, manipulation, and worse. It is also impor-tant to have a sense of respect for one's self. If self-image levels are low—if we feel unworthy of love from others, if we are so hungry for love that we are willing to take it from anyone who offers—then we become susceptible to giving in**

OPTIONS

LARGE GROUP

HEARD IT ALL BEFORE

LITTLE BIBLE BACKGROUND

MOSTLY GUYS

MEDIA

to the sexual urges we feel. Offer to talk with or recommend counseling to anyone who feels this way.

Your emotional state of mind can influence every decision you make. By committing right now to save sex for marriage, you can avoid a lot of needless emotional suffering in the meantime. I guarantee you'll be glad if you do.

Worth the Wait? (Part 2)

(Needed: The list you started in Session 1)

Explain that if sex were purely a physical act, it would be easier to cope with. But the emotions that accompany sexual activity are incredibly powerful. Have group members add to their list of reasons to save sex for marriage, this time focusing entirely on the emotional concerns that are involved. Among other things, they should come up with the following:

• You never have to worry about "getting caught." You can experience peace of mind rather than guilt, shame, and other horrible feelings.

• When you *do* get married, you will have a completely clear conscience and can give complete loyalty to your spouse.

• Your current relationships will be stronger (and probably longer).

Ask group members to recall any recent negative emotions they may have felt in regard to dating relationships. Close in prayer, asking God to remove the strong temptation to have sex, to heal any emotions that are painful, and to provide the strength for group members to make good decisions concerning their future sex lives.

The Gift

The gift sat in a distant corner with the tag in clear sight: "Do not open until Christmas." But Christmas seemed like such a long time away to Joe. The gift was from his favorite relative—the one who always gave the best presents on birthdays and holidays. Most relatives just gave cards, socks, or underwear, but this one gave wonderful, excellent, thrilling gifts. (And the relative had promised that this one would be the best yet.)

The gold foil wrapping and brightly colored bow made it quite a temptation to Joe. The gift looked mysterious and exciting from across the room, and the closer he got to it, the more exotic it appeared. Of course, he got all those warnings from his parents: "Be sure to leave the gift alone until it's the right time to open it." But time was *crawling*. Each hour seemed like a day, and each day seemed like a month.

One day Joe was at home alone while his parents were out shopping. No matter what he tried to do—homework, TV, or whatever—he seemed to end up in the same room with the gift. He wanted to know more about it. He just couldn't help it. He finally wandered closer and picked it up. It even *felt* exciting. He gave it a little shake and the sound from within was *so* tantalizing.

Joe happened to notice that it would be pretty easy to gently slip the bow off of the wrapping, carefully undo the tape at one end, slide the box out of the wrapping, and see exactly what the gift was. He struggled with the temptation, but finally resisted. He put the gift back down and returned to his homework. The thought of the gift kept crossing his mind, but he knew that was only natural. Anything so special was certain to command a lot of thought and attention.

Each time his parents were gone, he again felt the temptation to open the gift and see exactly what it was. But after he had made up his mind not to open the gift, it became a little bit easier to wait as he experienced each recurring temptation. His eagerness and anticipation increased, but he knew he could wait until Christmas came.

When Christmas *finally* arrived, Joe was handed the gift. The giver sat back and watched as Joe opened it. The moment was special for both of them. And, wow, Joe couldn't believe what a great gift it was! If he could have listed every single thing he wanted for Christmas, the whole list wouldn't have been half as good as this single gift.

The gift was something special that Joe treasured throughout his lifetime. He frequently thought back to that very special Christmas. Every time he did, the memory thrilled him. Very few other experiences in life would ever compare to what he felt that day. He was overjoyed that he had managed to wait until the time was right. And Joe—as well as the giver of the gift—lived happily ever after.

The Gift

The gift sat in a distant corner with the tag in clear sight: "Do not open until Christmas." But Christmas seemed like such a long time away to Joe. The gift was from his favorite relative—the one who always gave the best presents on birthdays and holidays. Most relatives just gave cards, socks, or underwear, but this one gave wonderful, excellent, thrilling gifts. (And the relative had promised that this one would be the best yet.)

The gold foil wrapping and brightly colored bow made it quite a temptation to Joe. The gift looked mysterious and exciting from across the room, and the closer he got to it, the more exotic it appeared. Of course, he got all those warnings from his parents: "Be sure to leave the gift alone until it's the right time to open it." But time was *crawling*. Each hour seemed like a day, and each day seemed like a month.

One day Joe was at home alone while his parents were out shopping. No matter what he tried to do—homework, TV, or whatever—he seemed to end up in the same room with the gift. He wanted to know more about it. He just couldn't help it. He finally wandered closer and picked it up. It even *felt* exciting. He gave it a little shake and the sound from within was *so* tantalizing.

Joe happened to notice that it would be pretty easy to gently slip the bow off of the wrapping, carefully undo the tape at one end, slide the box out of the wrapping, and see exactly what the gift was. He struggled with the temptation, and finally gave in. He gingerly opened the gift, and it was great! He quickly had it out of the box and was just starting to enjoy it when he thought he heard his parents. He rapidly bundled it back up, replaced the tape and the bow, and tried to act as if nothing had happened.

Each time his parents were gone, he again felt the temptation to open the gift and enjoy it. And since he had already done so, it became a little bit easier to give in to each recurring temptation. Funny thing, though—every time he opened the gift it seemed a little less exciting and a lot less special. He even began to lose his enthusiasm for Christmas to get here. What else was there to look forward to?

When Christmas *finally* arrived, Joe was handed the gift. The giver watched as he opened it. Joe suspected it was obvious to everyone else that the previously shiny foil had lost its luster and that the bow had become rather shabby looking. He tried to act surprised, but could not seem to show much enthusiasm. His disappointment seemed to rub off on the others, and this Christmas just didn't seem very special.

The gift was something that Joe kept throughout his lifetime. But it never seemed special to him. He frequently thought back and wondered how things would have been different if he hadn't ruined the surprise. He was disappointed—too late—that he hadn't waited until the time was right. And Joe and the giver of the gift were never quite as close after that Christmas.

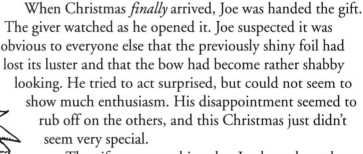

Step 3

Form teams. Give each team a supply of poster board and markers. Read Genesis 34 aloud in sections of two or three paragraphs at a time. At the end of each section, call out a number between 3 and 6. Each team must create a newspaper headline summarizing what happened in the section you just read, and the headline must have the number of words that you called out. The first team to complete its headline and carry it up to you wins that round.

Step 4

If reading the story on the Repro Resources would be too sedate or too difficult for your group, try another way to make a similar point. Before the session, put a fragile (but inexpensive) glass or ceramic figurine in a box. Don't try to protect the figurine with Styrofoam or other packing material. Wrap the box in wedding-gift paper. At this point in the session, play a lively game of floor hockey using the box as the puck. If you don't have hockey sticks or brooms, let kids use their feet. After playing for several minutes, stop the game. Carefully unwrap the figurine and give it as a "wedding present" to the group. Chances are it will be broken; even if it isn't, the box will be in bad shape. Use this as an illustration of the disappointing results of not keeping one's virginity intact as a wedding present for a spouse.

Step 1

If you don't have enough group members to manage the picture charades, here's another idea. Have kids stand next to each other in a line and hold hands. Anyone who lets go of anyone else's hand is out. Now have kids perform a variety of tasks, using only the hands that are clasped: eating popcorn; signing their names; drinking water from a paper cup; and defending themselves against a barrage of Ping-Pong balls or pillows that you throw. Then talk about how it felt to have such an "intimate" relationship (awkward, frustrating, interesting, etc.). Use this as an illustration of the fact that even physical relationships have an emotional side.

Step 2

If your pool of willing volunteers isn't large enough to act out one or more of the skits, try this. After describing only the second, third, and fourth situations, have kids write "love notes" from one character to the other, expressing feelings. For example, someone might write a note from Ted to Jane, apologizing for stretching the truth to the guys in the locker room. Someone else might write a note from Jeannie to Jason, expressing her fear of losing him. After sharing and discussing these notes, move to the summary at the end of the step, beginning with, **Sex is certainly a physical act. . . .**

Step 2

If your group is quite large, improvising skits can present two problems. First, if you have only a few kids putting on skits for the rest, the rest have nothing to do while the actors are preparing. Second, if you have everyone preparing skits, it takes too long to perform all of them (and kids are usually just waiting their turn to act, not paying attention to the other groups). Either way, you can lose the attention of those not performing. To remedy that, call the actors you need up to the front and have them pantomime as you read the situations one at a time (use just #2–#4). When you get to the end of a description, let the whole group suggest what the actors should say and do next. Rather than trying for smooth-running skits, let the actors try out different suggestions and let group members refine the results. Allow up to four minutes for each situation to be played out; then have actors summarize the emotions their characters experienced.

Step 5

To give as many kids as possible a chance to participate in discussion, form small groups at the start of this step. After asking each of the questions, let the small groups talk things over for a couple of minutes. When you get to the qualities associated with love in the Galatians passage, ask eight kids—each representing one of the qualities—to come to the front. Ask each to tell whether his or her quality would be more evident in a premarital sexual relationship, or in a relationship in which the couple is postponing sex until marriage—and why. Let other group members help out as needed.

Step 3

Cynical kids may laugh at the implication that premarital sex today always leads to violent revenge by family members as it did in Genesis 34. So instead of concluding the step with the summary statement in the basic session, ask kids to come up with a contemporary soap opera plot that includes all of the emotions (not the events) they listed from Genesis 34. The main characters should be a teenage guy and girl who have recently had sex. This activity should help ease the transition from the ancient example to today's application—that sex outside of marriage often leads to strong, negative emotions for those involved and those who care about them.

Step 5

Some kids may reject the claim that premarital sex is selfish and manipulative. If they know "nice" sexually active kids who've been going together for a long time, they may think it's possible to have a gentle, self-controlled, respectful, premarital sexual relationship. Arguing the point will prove fruitless, so approach the subject from a slightly different angle. After discussing whether sex is a good way to deepen love, turn the "why-wait-if-you're-in-love" question around: **What if you really love the other person? Why not wait in order to deepen your love?** Have half the group brainstorm ways in which having sex before marriage might deepen love; have the other half list ways in which waiting might deepen love. Share results. Then, rather than looking at the Galatians passage, read I Corinthians 13:4-8, concentrating on the last two verses. Point out that biblical love is an "always" thing. It involves a commitment to staying together no matter what. Waiting deepens that kind of love; *not* waiting shows that you're unwilling to make a binding commitment, which calls into question the claim that you're really in love.

Step 3

Kids with little Bible background may be confused by the customs and violence of Genesis 34. If you anticipate such a response from your group, look at Psalm 51 instead. David wrote this confession after being confronted about his adultery with Bathsheba (II Samuel 11:1—12:25). Ask kids to list emotions found in this Psalm (guilt, regret, sorrow, hope for forgiveness and restoration) and to suggest the kind of music that would best fit it. Also point out the other results of David's adultery—the murder of Bathsheba's husband as David tried to cover his tracks, and the death of David's infant son.

Step 5

If you use the Galatians passage, you may need to explain the "fruit of the Spirit" concept. Kids may assume that Galatians 5:22, 23 is simply a list of good qualities and that 5:19-21 is a list of bad ones. Point out that "fruit of the Spirit" is what God's Spirit grows in us when we belong to Christ and let Him change us. The fruit is the "produce" or product of the Spirit, the evidence that He's there. If these qualities are nowhere to be found in our lives, we need to ask whether God's Spirit is in us at all. If these qualities aren't showing in our dating relationships, we need to ask whether we're trying to keep God away from that part of our lives.

Step 1

To start the session with a relational activity, group kids according to the color of their shoes (or another arbitrary criterion such as birth month). Make sure each small group has at least two kids in it. Present each small group with the following problem, which its members must solve by consensus: **All the members of your small group want to go to college. But there's only enough money for one of you to go. If you share the money equally, none of you will get to go more than a semester. And if you don't go this year, it will be at least four years before you can try again. Who gets to go?** After a couple of minutes, ask kids what they decided. Chances are that no consensus was reached—or the decision was made and the left-out ones aren't happy. Point out that men and women who spend their lives together have to make tough decisions like this and live with the results. Having a superficial trait—shoe color, birth month, sexual attraction—in common isn't enough to form the kind of relationship that lasts through tough choices and hard times.

Step 6

Bring a guitar or other accompaniment. Point out that as the inventor of sex and emotions, God understands how the two work together. He reserves sexual activity for those who are married, not because He wants us to feel frustrated, but in part because He knows what premarital sex can do to people emotionally. Spend some time thanking God that He understands and values our feelings, sexual and otherwise. Then ask kids to suggest a few songs—anything from hymns to Top 40—that engage their emotions. Sing as many of the well-known ones as you have time for, reminding kids that God is Lord of our emotions in and out of church.

Step 2

You'll need to make some changes in the skits at the beginning of Step 2. For Skit #1, change the scenario so that Angie is the one who has never dated—and never even cared that much about dating. Her feelings about dating change, however, when she accepts Andrew's invitation to go to a football game with him. In the skit, Angie should be explaining her new feelings about dating to her friend Joan, who has never had a date. For Skit #2, change the scenario so that Jane is the one with several previous relationships. In the skit Jane should be trying to explain her real feelings about Ted to her friends, who only want to hear the "juicy" details of her dates. For Skit #3, ask a girl to play the role of Jason, and present the skit as it is written.

Step 4

After the discussion of Repro Resources 3 and 4, focus on the idea of sex being a gift. Ask for several volunteers to debate this question: **Are we the giver or the receiver of the gift of our own sexuality?** Have them consider the question particularly as it relates to the female perspective and responsibility in a dating relationship. After the debate has gone on for a few minutes, ask the following clarifying question: **Is sex ours to give away as we please—or have we received this gift from God and are accountable to use it as the Giver has requested, saving it for marriage?** Discuss how a person's answer to the question would affect her behavior.

Step 2

If you have a hard time coming up with actors for guy-girl skits, try this instead. Set out an assortment of "used" refreshments: chewed gum, half-eaten cookies, apples with bites taken out of them, etc. When kids are reluctant to partake, ask them why. Discuss how some kids have no problem with using each other sexually, but don't want "used" people when they're looking for a lasting relationship. **How might each of these "used" people feel: (a) a guy who is pressured by his friends to lose his virginity, only to get a girl pregnant when he does so; (b) a girl who "proves" her love by having sex, only to be dumped by the guy; (c) a guy who believed he was "safe" as long as he had "protection," only to get AIDS anyway; (d) a girl who hears her date from last night telling other guys that she was "really hot"?** Then move to the post-skit summary at the end of the step.

Step 5

Guys may ask the "what-if-you-love-each-other" question only in the interest of justifying what they really want: sex. Point this out by having them run an obstacle course in which the obstacles represent loving (but nonsexual) acts a guy could do for his girlfriend. Examples: running through a row of tires could stand for fixing a flat in the rain; walking several yards with a box over your head could stand for ignoring the charms of other girls; crawling on your knees could stand for praying together. After the race, discuss: **What percentage of guys do you think see the "finish line" of this race as getting to have sex? Do you think most guys would be willing to go through all this stuff without the "reward" of sex? On a list of the top ten truly loving things you could do for a girlfriend, where would sex be? Why?**

Step 1

Before the session, play any team game your kids like—softball, charades, Frisbee football, etc. Use conventional teams for the first five minutes. Then change the rules, allowing half the kids on each team to play without being committed to either side. These kids can switch loyalties anytime, moving from team to team depending on who's winning, where the sun is, etc. After playing this for another five minutes, stop the game. Ask: **How did the committed players feel about the uncommitted ones? How much interest could the uncommitted players have in who won the game?** Use this later in the session to illustrate the emotional strain placed on a relationship where partners are "playing around" but not "playing for keeps."

Step 6

If you have time for another game, try this. You'll need a lock and at least a dozen keys that look like they might fit the lock. Before the meeting, hide the keys around your meeting place so that they're tough to find. Hide the correct key in the toughest place of all. At this point in the session, turn kids loose to look for the right key. The first one to open the lock (if anyone does) will be the winner. Award a prize if you like. After the contest, discuss how frustrating it felt to search for the keys, only to be disappointed when they weren't the right ones. Make a parallel to the much greater emotional upheaval that accompanies going from one sexual relationship to another, looking in vain for true love.

Step 2
Before your meeting, enlist the help of a few group members to record the following lines of dialogue on audio tape. The lines should be read with as much feeling as possible.
• (miserable) "My life is over."
• (joyful) "This is great! I can hardly wait to see what's going to happen!"
• (angry) "How could you do such a thing? This is all your fault."
• (fearful) "I don't know what to do now. I'm scared."
• (smug) "Yeah, I'm pretty proud of myself."
• (amazed) "You did what?"
Instead of acting out the Step 2 situations in your meeting, read the description of each situation. After each, play all the taped lines of dialogue. Ask: **Which of these lines might be spoken in this situation? By whom? What feelings are being expressed?** Then move to the summary at the end of the step.

Step 5
Before the session, ask several group members to bring a tape of a favorite song that contains the word love. At this point in the session, after raising the question of whether being in love justifies having sex, play as many songs as you have time for. As kids listen, they should write down what they think each song means when it mentions the word love. Then share definitions and ask: **If love has so many different meanings, how can you know when you're "in love enough" to justify having sex?**

Step I
Replace Steps I and 2 with the following. You (or a kid who has strong self-esteem) will be a human pinball. The pinball wears an inner tube around his or her middle. The rest of the group gets to push him or her around for one minute, using only hands and touching only the inner tube. Kids also get to push the pinball around verbally, hurling insults (warn kids not to use vulgarity or racial slurs). Then make the point: The pinball was physically protected by the inner tube, but couldn't be protected emotionally from the insults. In the same way, "safe sex" precautions may seem to protect people physically, but can't protect against the emotional problems that often accompany premarital sex. As an example of such a problem, read just situation #3 from Step 2 and ask kids to name the emotions the characters might feel. Then move to the summary statement at the end of Step 2.

Step 3
Genesis 34 requires a lot of reading; use two shorter passages instead. Read Proverbs 6:32-35, which mentions some emotional results of illicit sex. Then read Song of Songs 1:1-4, which displays emotions from the right kind of sexual relationship. Contrast the two passages: **How does someone who has sex outside of marriage end up feeling?** (Destroyed, disgraced, shamed.) **Does sex outside marriage always lead to these feelings?** (Some may feel disgraced right away, others years later. Some people may not feel ashamed until they stand before God to be judged.) **How might family members feel?** (Jealous, furious, vengeful.) **What feelings accompany a healthy, married sexual relationship?** (Joy, excitement, passion, admiration, delight, etc.) To save more time, skip the reactions to the statements at the start of Step 4; go straight to using the story on the Repro Resources.

Step 2
Use the following two skit options:
**(1) Brahim is HIV positive from a sexual relationship he had at fourteen. Since then, he's had intercourse with many girls. He lived by the philosophy, "If I have to go, I'm taking other people with me." At age sixteen he joined the church and has not been sexually active since. However, Brahim and Shaniqua, the pastor's daughter, have fallen in love. Although Brahim and Shaniqua have promised not to have sex with each other, should Brahim tell her (and his past girlfriends) his secret?
(2) Ray and Dontae are good buddies in the youth group. They both seem like nice Christian boys, and are liked by all the girls. One day, Albert, another guy in the youth group, discovered that Ray and Dontae are gay. Albert is not sure what to do. On one hand, he wants to tell the other members of the group; on the other hand, he doesn't want to gossip. What should Albert do?**

Step 3
A controversial topic that will expand the discussion of Dinah's rape is that of sexual abuse. This is an undiscussed reality in a number of urban churches that affects one in three girls and one in seven boys before the age of eighteen. Ask group members' opinions on incest, harassment, battery, sexual assault, and stalkers. If you think it's appropriate, have each group member write on a piece of paper "yes" or "no" if he or she has been sexually abused. Instruct group members that if they want help with their situations they should write their initials on their papers. Explain that you will contact (privately and discreetly) those who write their initials. Do this only if you are willing to genuinely help.

Step 2

Junior highers often find it hard to improvise skits. And since most of the situations listed involve dating, younger kids may not relate to them. So here's an alternative. Pass out paper bags, one to each group member. You'll be describing some situations; kids are to show with their paper bags how the characters might feel. Kids can show embarrassment by putting the bags over their heads; they can show anger by blowing up and popping the bags; they can show happiness or sadness by using the bags as hand puppets and laughing or crying; they can show nausea or a mixture of intense emotions by pretending to use the sacks as "barf bags."

Situation #1: Ken discovers that the girl he has a crush on is already sexually involved with a much bigger, stronger guy. Situation #2: Maria's boyfriend keeps telling her that everybody else is having sex and they haven't yet, and he wants to know why. Situation #3: Nathan, who has borrowed a *Playboy* magazine from a guy at school, is looking at it in his room when his father walks in. Situation #4: Cathy "fooled around" with a guy for the first time a few weeks ago, and now she thinks she might be pregnant—but isn't sure. After discussing kids' reactions if they're willing, point out that talking about sex means talking about strong emotions, too.

Step 3

Condense the Genesis 34 Bible study by reading only verses 1-7 and 25-31. Rather than using small groups (which may flounder unless you have an adult leader guiding each group), read the verses aloud and ask kids to call out the emotions displayed in the passage as you read. Write these feelings on the board; ask kids to rate how strong each feeling was on a scale of 1 to 10, with 10 being the strongest.

Step 1

If picture charades and the "Love Indicator" seem too unsophisticated for your group, try this instead. Write the following list of emotions on the board: regret, joy, disappointment, fear, contentment, confusion, love, hate, sadness, happiness, anger, obsession, boredom, cynicism. Then display several notebooks and say: **These are the "love diaries" of some famous people. As I hold each one up, tell me which of the emotions on this list you would expect to show up most often in that diary.** Here are some celebrities whose names you might use in addition to those currently "hot" with your group: Magic Johnson, Madonna, Roy Rogers and Dale Evans, Adam and Eve. Ask kids to explain their answers. Use this activity to lead into a discussion of the unbreakable tie between sex and emotions.

Step 6

Rather than just listing some of the negative emotions that can result from premarital sex, help kids think through those feelings by using the following simulation. Form small groups. Say: **Your group is starting a new greeting card company. In the next five minutes, your job is to come up with a card that people could send to one of the following: (a) an unmarried teenage girl who's just discovered that she's pregnant; (b) a guy whose plans for college have just fallen through because he has to marry his pregnant girlfriend; (c) a girl who's just been dumped by her boyfriend after "proving" her love by having sex with him; (d) a guy who's just found out that he has AIDS; or (e) the parents of any of these kids.** Then have kids share their cards and discuss the emotions they identified. Ask: **On a scale of 1 to 10, with 10 being the toughest, how hard was it to be encouraging in these situations?**

Date Used:

Approx.
Time

Step 1: Picture This ... _____
o Small Group
o Fellowship & Worship
o Extra Fun
o Short Meeting Time
o Extra Challenge
Things needed:

Step 2: A Skit ... _____
o Small Group
o Large Group
o Mostly Girls
o Mostly Guys
o Media
o Urban
o Combined Junior High/High School
Things needed:

Step 3: Hitting below ... _____
o Extra Action
o Heard It All Before
o Little Bible Background
o Short Meeting Time
o Urban
o Combined Junior High/High School
Things needed:

Step 4: Name That ... _____
o Extra Action
o Mostly Girls
Things needed:

Step 5: The Logical ... _____
o Large Group
o Heard It All Before
o Little Bible Background
o Mostly Guys
o Media
Things needed:

Step 6: Worth the Wait ... _____
o Fellowship & Worship
o Extra Fun
o Extra Challenge
Things needed:

YOUR GOALS FOR THIS SESSION:

Choose one or more

☐ To help kids realize that much of their focus on sex initiates in their minds.

☐ To help kids understand how their thoughts tend to influence their actions.

☐ To help kids replace sinful sexual thoughts with more positive and productive ones.

☐ Other _____

How Come?

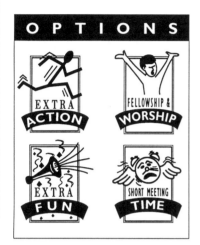

As soon as group members arrive, present them with a "How Come?" riddle. For example: **A man looks at the menu in a restaurant and sees that the special is porpoise. He has never ordered it before, so he decides to try it. When it arrives, he takes one bite, screams hysterically, and runs out of the restaurant. How come?**

Let kids ask yes-or-no questions until they arrive at the answer. (The man had been on a ship that wrecked on a remote island. Several people died. Food supplies were short. The ship's cook had served "porpoise" quite frequently until the survivors were eventually rescued. Yet with one taste in the restaurant, the man realized that what he had eaten on the island tasted nothing like the porpoise on his plate. ...)

Here's a less-extreme example (for more squeamish groups): **A man walks into a bar and asks for a glass of water. The bartender pulls out a gun and points it at the man. The man says "Thanks" and walks out. How come?** (He had hiccups and the bartender had successfully scared them out of him.)

[More of these "How Come" puzzles can be found in *Games* magazine, August 1992.]

Explain that most people enjoy mysteries and problem solving. Yet when the topic is sex, sometimes the mystery seems too much to understand. We have a natural curiosity about things we don't understand—especially sex. When we first discover how our physiology works, we tend to ask, "How come?" And it is normal to spend much of our teenage years thinking about sexual things.

STEP 2

Dear Abby

(Needed: Collection of advice column questions, pens, paper)

Try to deal with some of the specific "mysteries" of sex by reading a number of queries submitted to advice columnists. Teen magazines will probably provide some of the best examples. Select one of the questions, read it aloud, and let each group member write a short response. Collect the responses (which can remain anonymous) and read some of them aloud. Then compare their responses to the actual response from the columnist. In many cases your group members may discover that they know more than they thought. In fact their Christian perspective on many issues may actually provide better advice than a secular columnist.

After you let group members respond to a few questions from other young people, let *them* ask the questions. Again, keep it anonymous. Have them write down any questions they have about sex. Then collect the papers and read the questions at random, with no names attached. Be open and honest as you deal with the things they wish to know about sexual issues and/or relationships.

STEP 3

It's What's Inside That Counts

(Needed: Copies of Repro Resource 5, pens)

Explain that while some people tend to get caught up in "external" anatomy as they begin to think about sex, more concern should be given to two *internal* sex organs—the brain and the heart. Many young people spend endless hours trying to appear sexy on the outside. Millions of dollars are spent each year on acne creams, industrial strength deodorant, colognes and perfumes, hair products, makeup, clothes and accessories, and so forth—anything that might help make someone more attractive to the opposite gender. Yet if we focus more

on outward appearance than inner character, we do ourselves (and other people) a grave injustice.

Hand out copies of "Scrambled Wisdom" (Repro Resource 5), folded into thirds so each scrambled passage is on a separate third of the paper. Ask group members not to look at the first passage until you give the signal, and to not go on to the next one until you say so. Then let them work as individuals or in small groups to unscramble the passages one at a time. Don't let them look in their Bibles unless they absolutely can't figure out the passages. After each scrambled passage is solved, discuss what it means. The unscrambled passages are as follows:

• "I the Lord search the heart and examine the mind, to reward a man according to his conduct, according to what his deeds deserve" (Jeremiah 17:10). (God is aware of the things that go through our hearts and minds—both good and bad.)

• "Since, then, you have been raised with Christ, set your hearts on things above, where Christ is seated at the right hand of God. Set your minds on things above, not on earthly things" (Colossians 3:1, 2). (We choose the things we think about, and are capable of "setting our minds" on things that are godly rather than harmful for us.)

• "Do not conform any longer to the pattern of this world, but be transformed by the renewing of your mind. Then you will be able to test and approve what God's will is—his good, pleasing and perfect will" (Romans 12:2). (When we choose not to conform to the "regular" [worldly] way of thinking, God is able to transform and renew our thoughts.)

STEP 4

Horrible Thoughts, Horrible Actions

(Needed: Bibles)

To show how impure thoughts, when left unchecked, can lead to tragic results, have group members read the story of Amnon and Tamar in II Samuel 13:1-22. (If you have already done Session 1 as a group, explain that this is not the same Tamar as in the Genesis 38 account.) Depending on the maturity level of your group, you can either have volunteers read aloud, section by section, or have everyone read silently and then discuss the content.

II Samuel 13:1-6

Do you understand how the people in this story are re-

lated, and what the problem was between them? (Absalom and Tamar were children of King David. Amnon was also David's son [his oldest], but by a different mother. Jonadab was a cousin of the three children. Amnon was in "love" with Tamar, his half-sister, but marriage between them was forbidden under their law [Leviticus 20:17].)

Why do you think Amnon was "frustrated to the point of illness" (vs. 2)**?** (Perhaps because he continued to dwell on his misplaced "love" until it became an obsession. Rather than yield to God's law, he kept his mind focused on improper possibilities.)

What made Amnon's problem even worse? (He listened to an untrustworthy source of information. He found someone who told him what he wanted to hear, and acted on bad advice.)

Can you think of a recent time when you had a problem and kept asking around until you found someone who told you what you wanted to hear? What were the results?
II Samuel 13:7-14

Do you know people who remind you of Amnon in the way they think? (Some people seem to be consumed with thinking about sex [and potential encounters] all the time. They plot and plan and hope for any opportunity, without much thought about the potential consequences of their actions.)

What kind of person do you think Tamar was? Why? (She vehemently tried to protect her purity. *Her* mind seems to have been filled with logic, intelligence, and common sense.)

What appeals did Tamar make in attempting to convince Amnon to leave her alone? (She brought up her own purity, Amnon's reputation, and the legal aspects of his intended action; she even came up with a possible solution to the situation that wouldn't have involved sin or violence.)

Tamar made a lot of sense. Why do you think Amnon didn't listen to her? (He had one selfish goal, and he didn't care what he had to do to accomplish it. Perhaps his mental fantasies were so powerful that he refused to miss this opportunity.)
II Samuel 13:15-22

Do you think Amnon's "love" for Tamar was genuine? Why? (His feelings for her proved to be merely lust, or he wouldn't have "hated her more than he had loved her" [vs. 15] after he forced her to have sex.)

How did Tamar's response differ from Amnon's? (Her remorse was genuine. Amnon should have married her after raping her, even though his reputation would have been affected [Deuteronomy 22:28, 29]. *Her* reputation was destroyed. Not only did she have to suffer through Amnon's rape, but his refusal to marry her meant she wasn't likely to *ever* find a husband due to the cultural stigma of the time.)

King David was "furious" when he heard what had hap-

pened, but why do you think he didn't punish Amnon for his actions? (Perhaps David recalled his own recent affair with Bathsheba [II Samuel 11], which had resulted in adultery, deceit, and the eventual murder of Bathsheba's husband. It would have been difficult for him to chastise his son for doing something so similar to what he himself had done.)

Explain that Amnon didn't go unpunished for long, however. Tamar's full brother, Absalom, waited two years for the right opportunity, and had Amnon killed. As a result, David not only lost Amnon as a son, but Absalom ran away and eventually became a major adversary to David (II Samuel 13:23-39).

When fantasies go unchecked, the results are not always what we think. It was certainly true for Amnon. It took only one actual sexual encounter to destroy his "love," the girl's reputation, the stability of his family, and even his life. We should learn from his experience the importance of not allowing ourselves to be consumed by mental fantasies.

STEP

5

Lust Busters

(Needed: Bibles, copies of Repro Resource 6)

OPTIONS

EXTRA ACTION

LARGE GROUP

HEARD IT ALL BEFORE

MOSTLY GIRLS

MOSTLY GUYS

MEDIA

Where do fantasies come from? (Most people have a natural curiosity about sex when they get to a certain age. But as they begin to try to satisfy that curiosity, many people let it become an obsession. At this point, some look for answers in pornographic publications.)

Is it wrong to think a lot about sex? (It depends. There is certainly nothing wrong with getting the facts and gathering enough information to make wise decisions. But dwelling on the topic can possibly lead to lust, disrespect for the other gender as a whole, and an inability to think clearly and rationally. And for those involved with pornography, it is very difficult to remove or ignore the mental images that have been formed. Thinking about sex isn't necessarily wrong, but *lust* is.)

Why do you think teenagers think about sex so much? (Their bodies are changing, which initiates normal questions; it's a popular topic of discussion; they are exposed to vast amounts of sexual material in ads, TV shows, and movies; etc.)

Hand out copies of "It's All in Your Head" (Repro Resource 6). Let group members determine which of the items listed they would classify as "things of beauty," which would be "objects of lust," and which would be somewhere in between. When they finish, discuss their responses.

Then discuss: **Suppose you're standing on the beach and see two people pass you going in opposite directions. One is a girl in a thong bathing suit, or guy in Speedo trunks. The other looks very much the same, but is dressed more modestly. Which one would your eyes follow down the beach? Why?** It is hoped that group members wouldn't be trying to pick up *any* stranger off the beach; yet many might confess to paying more attention to the skimpily clothed person. They may even have some good reasons to try to justify their actions.

Would you consider your attitude "lustful"? Why?

What if you were the modestly clothed person and were rejected simply because someone else was more naked than you were? How would you like to be evaluated purely on how little you wear or how good your body looked?

Do you think it's OK to pay more attention to people who "turn you on," or do you think it's wrong to do so? (It's a form of judging others on appearance. And while it's a natural reaction, Christians should have the "supernatural" goal of not showing favoritism for any reason—race, gender, age, or cut of a bathing suit.)

Summarize: **Lust is one of the hardest emotions to cope with. We want to think that other people like us and find us attractive. But if we keep going and begin to dwell on what kind of wonderful lovers we would be, we've gone too far. And if we don't do something to control those thoughts, we may one day find ourselves with the opportunity to do something, and without the resistance to stop.**

So in conclusion, let us repeat the Lustbusters Code. Repeat after me. (Stop at marked intervals and let group members echo your words.) **Whatever is true/ whatever is noble/ whatever is right/ whatever is pure/ whatever is lovely/ whatever is admirable/ if anything is excellent or praiseworthy/ think about such things/ And the God of peace will be with you/ Philippians 4:8, 9.**

In a world filled with 976 numbers for sexual fantasy and sensual pleasure, challenge group members to memorize the 489 number (Philippians 4:8, 9). As they replace lustful thoughts with pure ones on a regular basis, they will see inevitable changes in their attitudes and behaviors as well. Have them memorize the verses at this point in the session if time permits.

Worth the Wait? (Part 3)

(Needed: The list you worked on in Sessions 1 and 2)

Conclude by having group members think of additional reasons to save sex for marriage, this time based on the intellectual/mental aspects of sex. This will probably be a bit harder to do than the physical or emotional aspects were, but group members should be able to come up with a few good reasons. Alert them that sexual activity tends to consume one's thoughts, as well as his or her emotional energy. Consequently, by committing to postpone sex until marriage:

• you find more efficient uses for your mental time and energy;

• you are able to focus better on schoolwork, jobs, etc;

• you find that abstinence is a source of creative power. Rather than dwelling on the lust involved in sexual desire, you can develop other ways to express your powerful feelings (songs, poems, plays, etc.).

Explain that as pleasant as romance and sexual things can be to think about, sex can have a powerful way of consuming our mental energy if we don't watch out. If bad habits have already been formed in this area, it may be hard to break them. But it is a freeing experience to take control of our thoughts and learn once more how to think about a variety of worthwhile and productive things.

SCRAMBLeD
W I S D O M

The words of the following verses have been taken out of order and alphabetized. It's up to you to restore them to their proper places—without using your Bibles. When you think you have the solution, have your leader check it. Don't go on to the next verse until you are told to do so.

PASSAGE #1 (One sentence)

a / according / according / and / conduct, / deeds / deserve" / examine / heart / his / his / "I / Lord / man / mind, / reward / search / the / the / the / to / to / to / what / (Jeremiah 17:10).

PASSAGE #2 (Two sentences)

above / above, / at / been / Christ, / Christ / earthly / God. / hand / have / hearts / is / minds / not / of / on / on / on / raised / right / seated / Set / set / "Since, / the / then, / things / things / things" / where / with / you / your / your / (Colossians 3:1, 2).

PASSAGE #3 (Two sentences)

able / and / and / any / approve / be / be / but / by / conform / "Do / God's / good, / his / is— / longer / mind. / not / of / of / pattern / perfect / pleasing / renewing / test / the / the / Then / this / to / to / transformed / what / will / will / will" / world, / you / your / (Romans 12:2).

It's All in Your Head

If you are a teenager, and if all teenagers think a lot about sex, what does that say about you? But, hey, thinking about sex isn't necessarily wrong. It's normal and natural to have a lot of thoughts and questions about something so powerful and mysterious. Yet if those thoughts shift to mental images of you and a boyfriend or girlfriend doing all sorts of unmentionable things, your curiosity has turned to lust. Curiosity is fine. Lust is a sin.

Sometimes our tendencies to lust can be initiated by certain things. And what causes some people to lust can draw yawns out of other people. So for each of the items listed below, indicate whether you admire it for its pure aesthetic beauty, despise it as an object of lust, or would rate it somewhere in between.

A THING _____ AN OBJECT
OF BEAUTY   OF LUST
The Venus de Milo (or Michelangelo's David)

A THING _____ AN OBJECT
OF BEAUTY   OF LUST
A friend's baby pictures (naked on a shag rug)

A THING _____ AN OBJECT
OF BEAUTY   OF LUST
Madonna's *Sex* book

A THING _____ AN OBJECT
OF BEAUTY   OF LUST
A real babe in a string bikini (or a hunk in a Speedo swimsuit)

A THING _____ AN OBJECT
OF BEAUTY   OF LUST
Naked tribespeople in *National Geographic*

A THING _____ AN OBJECT
OF BEAUTY   OF LUST
Lingerie models in the Victoria's Secret catalog

A THING _____ AN OBJECT
OF BEAUTY   OF LUST
Miss (Mr.) November from *Plaything* magazine

A THING _____ AN OBJECT
OF BEAUTY   OF LUST
R-rated movies (love stories)

A THING _____ AN OBJECT
OF BEAUTY   OF LUST
"Adult" movies on cable

A THING _____ AN OBJECT
OF BEAUTY   OF LUST
A nude model in a college art class

A THING _____ AN OBJECT
OF BEAUTY   OF LUST
A soap opera scene between two very good-looking people

EXTRA ACTION

Step 1

Instead of the riddles, try this game. Form two teams. Each team is supposed to memorize a Bible verse. But every 15 seconds or so, tell one team to get up and run in a circle around the other, yelling the lyrics from a song of its choosing. After three minutes, see which team did a better job of memorizing its verse (have kids recite it one word at a time, taking turns). Tie this into the difficulty of concentrating when our minds are frequently interrupted by sexual thoughts. For more action in Step 2, skip the advice columns and have kids pantomime (for their teams to guess) the following ways in which some people try to get their questions about sex answered: watching a steamy video; sneaking into a theater to watch an R-rated movie; peeking at "skin" magazines in a convenience store; listening to jokes in the locker room; asking a parent; going to health class; checking out a library book. Then discuss which sources are most and least reliable.

Step 5

To determine who answers the discussion questions in this step, have kids pass a foam rubber ball from person to person. Whoever is touching the ball when you finish asking a question has to answer it. Anyone who refuses to answer must recite the "Lustbusters Code" after you (see end of Step 5).

SMALL GROUP

Step 2

The smaller the group, the more reluctant kids may be to write down their own sexual questions and hand them in. It's pretty easy to guess who asked a question when there are just a few kids. So after using the advice columns, ask: **On a scale of 1 to 10—with 10 being the highest—how curious do you think most kids your age are about the following questions, and why?**
• **Where do babies come from?**
• **How can I stop thinking about sex so much?**
• **How can I keep from getting (or getting a girl) pregnant?**
• **What do people of the opposite sex look like naked?**
• **How far can I go without getting in trouble?**
Let kids suggest and rate other questions if they're willing.

Step 6

Brainstorming can be hard when you have just a few kids and their brains aren't storming at the moment. Prime the idea pump by having kids list at least twenty things they could think about in a 10-minute period. Be sure to write the words "a sexual fantasy" somewhere on the list. Then ask what kind of positive, practical value could result from having thought about each item. Which "trains of thought" are a waste of time? What might we miss by spending too much time thinking about sex?

LARGE GROUP

Step 2

Trying to read the advice-column replies and answer the questions kids submit may take too long in a large group. Instead, form five teams. Each team answers the advice-column question from a different perspective: Team 1 is a doctor or psychologist; Team 2 is a nervous parent; Team 3 is a kid who thinks he or she knows all about sex but doesn't; Team 4 is a comedian; Team 5 is a pastor. After a few minutes, share and discuss results. Skip the submission of real sexual questions unless you're prepared to deal with them in depth at a future meeting.

Step 5

To give more kids a chance to discuss the questions, break into small groups. Read a question (for example, **Why do you think teenagers think about sex so much?**) aloud; give groups one minute to discuss it, and then ask for reports. Work your way through the questions and the Repro Resource in this way.

HEARD IT ALL BEFORE

Step 3
Instead of doing the unscrambling activity, establish *why* it's important to filter out certain thoughts. Display several kinds of filters (oil, air, water, furnace, gasoline, etc.). See whether kids can guess what they filter out and what they leave in. Discuss the damage the filtered-out dirt, germs, or other impurities could have done if they weren't removed. Use this as an illustration of the practical value of keeping our minds clean to avoid damage (warped ideas and expectations about sex, gross images that keep coming back when we don't want them to, etc.) over the long haul.

Step 5
The word *lust* sounds old-fashioned, even comical, to many kids today. If you're going to use it, define it first: **Lust isn't just any stray thought about sex that might flit through your mind. To lust is to set your heart on something, long for, covet it** (want to possess it even though it belongs to someone else). Also, kids may have heard Philippians 4:8, 9 oversold as the "antidote" to "dirty thoughts." Instead of reciting the "Lustbusters Code," try a different tack: ask what is true, noble, right, pure, lovely, etc. about *sex*. For example, something true about sex: It's not all there is to life. Something right about sex: It's fine within marriage. Something praiseworthy: God's design of the reproductive system is pretty amazing.

LITTLE BIBLE BACKGROUND

Step 3
The verse-unscrambling activity will be hard enough for kids who have heard the verses—impossible for those who haven't. Try this instead: Draw the outline of a human body on chalkboard or poster board. Have kids read the verses and add to the picture any body parts that are mentioned (mind [brain] and heart.) Explain that "heart" was used to refer to the source of emotions and motivations, the most personal inner part of ourselves. Using the picture, point out that God sees through surface qualities to the way we really are inside.

Step 4
You may want to replace the II Samuel study with the shorter and simpler Genesis 39:6-10, the story of Joseph and Potiphar's wife (see "Combined Junior High/High School" option). If you prefer to stick with Amnon and Tamar, explain that in verse 13, Tamar is reminding Amnon that raping her could keep him from becoming king; her suggestion that David would let them get married probably was a desperation move, since such a marriage was illegal. Verse 16 refers to the fact that as an ex-virgin, Tamar couldn't be offered by her father as anyone else's bride-to-be. The ashes and robe-tearing in verse 19 were signs of mourning.

FELLOWSHIP & WORSHIP

Step 1
Instead of using the riddles, break the group into pairs. Have partners discuss approximately how old they were when they did the following, and how they felt about each event:
• learned how to tie their shoes;
• stayed overnight away from home;
• sent or received a valentine; and
• started wondering where babies come from.

Step 6
Read Philippians 4:8, 9 again. Hand out eight sheets of poster board to small groups or individuals. On each sheet should be written one of the qualities (true, noble, right, etc.) from the passage. Each person or group should come up with ten things that have that quality and that are present right now in your meeting place. This could include people, attitudes, actions, or things. Then share results. Make sure kids understand that God's gift of sexuality belongs on each list. Spend some time thanking God for the things on your lists.

Step 4

After reading and discussing the events that took place in Tamar's life, talk about what might be different if the events had occurred in today's culture. Then ask: **Do you think God's attitude toward Tamar changed because of these experiences? Why or why not?**

Step 5

Have group members form teams of four or five. Distribute paper and pencils to each team. Instruct each team to write a response to this statement: **Some say that "lust" is not as much a temptation for girls as it is for guys. If your team agrees with this statement, write down some suggestions for what you can do to help your guy friends. If your team disagrees with this statement, write down some suggestions for what you can do to help yourselves and your guy friends.**

Step 2

Skip the verse-unscrambling activity and go directly to two Bible passages that deal specifically with the temptations felt by young men. Read Psalm 119:9-11 and ask: **Do you think it's tougher for a guy to "keep his way pure" than it is for a girl? Why or why not? If a guy were "living according to [God's] word," what would be his attitude toward sexual fantasies? Without the motivation shown in verses 10 and 11, how do you think a guy will do in a battle to control sexual thoughts? If you've tried hiding God's Word in your heart, what happened?** Then read I Timothy 5:1, 2. Ask: **If all guys treated all girls "as sisters, with absolute purity," what would happen? How might this apply to the way a guy treats a girlfriend?** (He should respect her and stay away from sexual activity before marriage.) **How could it apply to the way guys think of the girls they see?** (Guys should think of girls as complete human beings, not sex objects; as people to be cared for, not used.)

Step 5

They probably won't say it, but your guys may feel such hormonal pressure that most of the items listed on Repro Resource 6 could arouse them—unless they've been jaded by frequent exposure to the more explicit ones. Having to admit this to themselves may just make them feel abnormal. Consider skipping the sheet and spending more time at the end of the step discussing which stores, radio stations, TV channels, and other potential sexual stimulants guys should avoid if they want to make temptation-fighting easier.

Step 1

Bring a bunch of nylon stockings. Choose several "beauty pageant" contestants (both sexes) to parade before a panel of judges. Have all contestants wear the stockings over their heads, messing up their features. Ask the panel to choose winners in categories like Most Alluring, Most Likely to Rob a Bank, etc. Then ask whether wearing stockings over our heads would cut down on the number of "lustful" thoughts in the world. Would wearing baggier clothes help? If not, what do kids think is the answer to out-of-control sexual thoughts?

Step 6

Provide a Polaroid camera, film, and a three-foot length of rope. Have kids pose in threes, with two kids using "mental floss" on the third—looking as if they're pulling the rope back and forth through the person's ears, cleaning out his or her brain. Encourage kids to ham it up, and to make the through-the-head illusion look as real as possible. Take enough pictures so that each group member gets one of himself or herself being "flossed." Have kids take the pictures home as a reminder of what you've discussed.

Step 2

Bring a video camera, a flip chart, and a marker. Have kids put together a fake "health class film" called *The Birds and the Bees*, giving made-up explanations of where babies come from. (Examples: babies grow on trees; they come from vending machines; they're really dolls that have been exposed to radioactivity, etc.) Then play the video back to the group. Follow with a discussion on the kinds of sexual questions kids *really* want answered.

Step 5

Set up a Nintendo or other video game and let kids play it for a round or two. Then liken the game to fighting sexual temptation. Have kids rename the parts of the game (weapons used, obstacles to overcome, traps, goal, etc.) to make it reflect the battle against out-of-control sexual thoughts. For instance, a weapon might be renamed "memorized Bible verses"; a trap might be labeled "too much time alone" or "watching old Madonna videos." Then have kids play the game with the new labels in mind.

Step 1

For a shorter opener, replace Steps 1 and 2 with the following. Bring a package that you've put in a plain, brown wrapper and on which you've written "Adults Only" in large letters. Set the package at the front of the room and let kids ask yes-or-no questions until they guess what's in it (or until three minutes have passed). Then unwrap the package to reveal a jar of denture cleanser or another "senior citizen" item. Acknowledge that it's normal for kids to be curious about things that are for "adults only"—including sex. To save more time, skip the unscrambling activity in Step 3 and just read the verses.

Step 4

For a shorter Bible study, see the "Combined Junior High/High School" option for Step 4. Or stick with II Samuel 13:1-22 and ask only the following questions: **Did Amnon really love Tamar? What should he have done about his fantasies? At what point did his thoughts turn to action? How might Tamar answer those who think sexual fantasies are no big deal?** To save time in Step 5, skip the discussion after the Repro Resource and jump to the summary (**Lust is one of the hardest emotions to cope with …**).

Step 2

After your group members give feedback on the magazine queries, tell them you will read old love letters of yours from the past. The love letters are actually from the Song of Solomon (Songs). On crumpled-up pieces of paper write portions of chapters 1-4. (Make gender changes where needed.) Begin each portion with "Dear_____." After reading nostalgically four separate letters, reveal to your group members that the letters are actually from the Bible. Explain that Solomon's description of his love has been used to describe Christ's love for the church.

Step 3

Teaching that internal beauty is much more desirable than external beauty is key. A great way to do this is to post a picture of Mother Teresa and a picture of Madonna. Then ask: **Don't you think Mother Teresa is more beautiful than Madonna?** Group members will probably respond with statements like "Are you blind?" and "You need glasses!" That's OK. Ask them to explain their reactions. Then help them see that beauty is much more than sexiness and "looks." Sexuality is ultimately an attitude of the spirit, so that even if people choose a celibate lifestyle, they will be sexually fulfilled in Christ. Have someone read aloud I Samuel 16:7. Then have each group member make two signs, one that says "Outward Beauty" and one that says "Inward Beauty." Then have group members tape each sign next to the appropriate picture. Madonna will probably receive the most "Outward Beauty" votes. But remind group members that the category that is important to God is "Inward Beauty." So Mother Teresa wins!

Step 2

Younger kids may be at a loss as to how to answer advice column questions, especially those that deal with sexual specifics. Instead, cut the questions and answers apart, give each person at least one question and answer, and have kids mingle and match questions with answers. Then let kids give thumbs up or down on the advice contained in the ones they matched.

Step 4

For younger kids, the story of Amnon and Tamar may be too long and may raise more questions than it answers. Instead, read part of the story of Joseph and Potiphar's wife (Genesis 39:6-10). Ask: **How does this story show that out-of-control sexual thoughts can be a problem for girls as well as guys? How could Mrs. Potiphar have reacted to Joseph's good looks instead of having fantasies about him? How did Joseph try to get Mrs. Potiphar's mind off fantasies and back to reality? How could we do the same thing when thoughts like these bother us? Mrs. Potiphar's thoughts just ended up frustrating her and driving Joseph away. How do our own sexual thoughts affect us and other people?**

Step 3

Older kids may find the verse-unscrambling exercise "beneath" them, and three passages may not be necessary to convince them that God is interested in their thoughts. If you think that's the case in your group, look at two other passages instead: Matthew 5:27, 28 and Romans 1:21-32. Concerning the Matthew passage, ask: **How do you think men felt when they heard this? How about women? Why do you think Jesus was as interested in thoughts as in actions?** (God knows our thoughts; thoughts often lead to action; God wants purity inside and out.) Regarding the Romans passage, ask: **How are lustful thoughts futile and foolish** (vs. 21), **degrading** (vs. 24), **and shameful** (vs. 26)? **How are wrong sexual thoughts part of the "bigger picture" of the way people relate to God?** (Many people have rejected God, so He has let them go ahead and live the way they want to. The includes having sexually immoral thoughts as well as the sins listed in verses 29-31.)

Step 6

Instead of just encouraging kids to stop fantasizing sexually, challenge them to come up with specific ways to break such a habit. For example, what mental images could kids call up as "alarms" that go off when lustful thoughts are first detected? (A fire engine, a computer "bomb" icon, etc.) What mental "stepping stones" could kids take from fantasy to reality? (Remembering that a lusted-after girl is someone's daughter; imagining Jesus walking onto the scene, etc.) So that kids will share these suggestions for each other's benefit, make it clear that you're not asking what each person will do to combat his or her problem; you're asking for ideas that could help anyone.

Date Used: _____

Approx. Time

Step 1: How Come? _____
o Extra Action
o Fellowship & Worship
o Extra Fun
o Short Meeting Time
Things needed:

Step 2: Dear Abby _____
o Small Group
o Large Group
o Mostly Guys
o Media
o Urban
o Combined Junior High/High School
Things needed:

Step 3: It's What's ... _____
o Heard It All Before
o Little Bible Background
o Urban
o Extra Challenge
Things needed:

Step 4: Horrible ... _____
o Little Bible Background
o Mostly Girls
o Short Meeting Time
o Combined Junior High/High School
Things needed:

Step 5: Lust Busters _____
o Extra Action
o Large Group
o Heard It All Before
o Mostly Girls
o Mostly Guys
o Media
Things needed:

Step 6: Worth the Wait ... _____
o Small Group
o Fellowship & Worship
o Extra Fun
o Extra Challenge
Things needed:

Sex and Other God-Honoring Things

YOUR GOALS FOR THIS SESSION:

Choose one or more

☐ To help kids see why God demands sexual purity prior to marriage.

☐ To help kids discover a connection between sexual purity and spiritual purity.

☐ To help kids experience complete forgiveness for any previous sexual sin, and to commit to abandoning any sinful habits that have been developed.

☐ Other _____

Your Bible Base:

Numbers 25:1-15
Hosea 1–3
1 Corinthians 6:15-17

Common Bonds

(Needed: Pens, copies of Repro Resource 7)

Divide into teams and hand out copies of "Three of a Kind" (Repro Resource 7). Ask group members not to look at the sheets until your signal. Before beginning, give them an example: **What do these three things have in common: birds, bats, and hospitals?** (They all have *wings*.)

Group members should work on the sheets individually or in groups to try to determine what each set of items has in common. The answers to the groupings on the sheet are:

(1) Kinds of snakes

(2) Things in banks

(3) Things with keys

(4) Words that come after "snow"

(5) Words found in recipes

(6) Things with blades

(7) "French" things

(8) Famous threesomes

(9) Things with rings

(10) Things with diamonds

(11) Things that have knots

(12) Tennis terms

(13) Types of sandwiches

(14) Types of cars

(15) Groups of animals (murder of crows, pride of lions, and school of fish)

After you've gone over the answers for the groupings on the sheet, give group members one more common bond to determine—a biblical one. Ask: **What do these people have in common: Rahab, Samson, and David?** If group members have trouble coming up with an answer, give them a clue by reminding them that this session is about sex. (All three were people who at one time gave in to their hormones and committed some serious sexual sins, yet who went on to do great things for God.) More people could be listed, but these three are all included in the list of "Heroes of the Faith" in Hebrews 11 (vss. 31, 32). As you go through this session and compare sexual purity with spiritual purity, start with this reminder that God is quick to forgive sexual sin if people are willing to repent.

STEP

2

Don't Take My Wife—Please

(Needed: Copies of Repro Resource 8)

The purpose of this session is to compare sexual purity with spiritual purity. Throughout history, God has tried to help us understand His love and devotion for humankind by comparing His relationship with us to the relationship between a husband and wife. Such relationships are supposed to be marked by mutual trust, faithfulness, love, loyalty, and so forth. But God's people have repeatedly turned their backs on His love as they chased after other gods—many times even while continuing to receive His blessings. The Bible story that follows will show that while God does not always choose to act immediately when we are sexually (and spiritually) unfaithful, He doesn't take our indiscretions lightly. One time He tried to let us know how He feels when we are disloyal to Him by allowing one of His prophets to experience a bit of the same grief.

Hand out copies of "My Unfaithful Wife: I Think I'll Keep Her" (Repro Resource 8). This is a somewhat lighthearted look at the love life of Hosea (based loosely on Hosea 1–3). Assign a guy to read the Hosea part and a girl to read the Gomer part; have everyone else read the People part together. At the end, ask group members to complete the skit by offering advice on how to avoid sexual/spiritual unfaithfulness.

Then ask: **If God had called on you instead of Hosea, would you have done what He asked? Why?**

If you had committed yourself to someone you knew was likely to be unfaithful and did all you could to love the person, and he or she deserted you anyway, do you think you would ever take the person back? If not, why not? If so, under what conditions?

What do you think was God's point for having Hosea go through this hard experience? (It's hard to think in terms of "cheating on" God. But when we see the same thing take place between a husband and wife, we can better understand the pain, betrayal, and other feelings that are involved. And if we can learn from Hosea and Gomer, we need not make the same, or similar, mistakes.)

OPTIONS

SMALL GROUP

LITTLE BIBLE BACKGROUND

MOSTLY GIRLS

MOSTLY GUYS

JR. HIGH HIGH SCHOOL COMBINED

STEP 3

The Cozbi Show

(Needed: Bibles)

At this point, challenge your group members with some viewpoints that they're probably hearing from some of their friends. Ask: **Is sexual sin really that big a deal? We've already said that some of God's greatest heroes—including David and Samson—were sexually active outside of marriage. And in today's society, the majority of people have premarital sex. How bad can it be?**

Let group members discuss their opinions (and represent those of their sexually active friends). Encourage them to be as convincing as possible in trying to prove that maybe, just maybe, the expectations of Christian parents and leaders are a little too high and/or unrealistic when it comes to refraining from premarital or extramarital sex. Then have everyone read Numbers 25:1-15 individually. Discuss:

What did the Israelites do that got God so angry at them? (The first obvious answer might be their *sexual* entanglements with the Moabites. Even more important, however, is how easily the Israelites abandoned their own *religious* "commitments" when a little easy sex became available.) Point out that the Israelites had repeatedly been warned not to have *any* involvement with the heathen people in the land of Canaan. (See Deuteronomy 7:1-6, for example.)

Explain that sex was a part of "worship" by the Moabites and other people who did not follow God. They practiced fertility rites regularly. Then ask: **Why do you think so many of the Israelites were quick to abandon their worship of the true God?** If no one mentions it, point out that personal gratification is so important to some people that any kind of spiritual discipline only seems to get in the way. People are no different today than during this time in Israel's history. If we limit our attention to the here-and-now, it's easy to make the same kind of mistake the Israelites made. But our commitment to God is eternal, and the faithfulness we show now will be rewarded in eternity.

What do young people do today that may be similar to the worship of Baal in this passage? (In order to impress a date, Christians sometimes start drinking, get involved with drugs, go farther [sexually] than they are comfortable with, and so forth. In addition, they may also stop going to church regularly—either out of guilt or because their new romantic interests deprive them of the time and energy previously put into spiritual commitment.)

Do you think the solution to this problem was a bit severe in the case of Zimri and Cozbi? It may seem so to your group members. After all, if the same penalty was applied in today's society, our population would immediately dwindle to a small percentage of what it is now. But point out the brazenness of this couple who came into the Israelite camp—interrupting those who were mourning the situation.

Do you think God has "softened His position" on sexual sin in recent years? If not, why do you think it is so wide-spread today? (Scripture is clear that people who commit sexual sin will eventually face judgment. Yet God desires that we turn from *all* of our sins—sexual sins included—and experience His love and forgiveness [II Peter 3:9].)

[Note: This is probably not the right time to bring it up, but this is a good passage to recall when you're asked why God commanded the Israelites to annihilate the nations they encountered—women and all. While it seems cruel, God knew the weaknesses of His people. The Israelites were much too quick to abandon God when faced with the opportunity to participate in the sexual/religious practices of other gods.]

STEP

4

Representatives

(Needed: The name of each group member written on an individual slip of paper)

Explain that there is another reason why sexual activity is so related to spiritual things. To demonstrate, hand everyone a folded slip of paper that contains the name of a person in the group. Everyone present should have someone else's name. Then ask a number of opinion questions, and have people answer as if they were the person on the slip of paper. Here are some questions you could use:

• **What is one of your favorite sports?**
• **What would you say are your best characteristics?**
• **What do you think would be an appropriate nickname for you?**
• **When you face a conflict situation, are you more likely to run and hide, fight, or look for a compromise?**

• **Who do you think is the best-looking person in this group?**

• **Who in this group would you most like to date?**

• **How would you describe your feet?**

Try to have some fun with this, but not at the expense of someone's feelings. While you should expect some comical answers, don't allow group members to become cruel in their comments about the people they are representing.

Keep asking questions until it becomes clear who most of the group members are representing. Then discuss: **How did you like it when someone else got to answer personal questions on your behalf?** Were group members embarrassed? Angry? Frustrated?

How did it feel to represent someone else? Did group members try to be straightforward? Did they respond in an attempt to evoke a response from the person being represented?

Name some of the people or organizations that you actually "represent." (Schools, clubs, teams, bands, families, etc.)

How important is it to be a good representative of each of these groups?

Have someone read aloud I Corinthians 6:15-17. Discuss: **What does it mean that "[our] bodies are members of Christ Himself"?** (Each Christian has specific gifts and a responsibility to use those gifts for the good of the church as a whole [the "body" of Christ].)

How does it feel to know that you represent Jesus in everything you do? (It may be a bit overwhelming for many people. Yet it is also a tremendous privilege. While very few people in the group might be willing to be represented by another person, Jesus Himself trusts *us* with that responsibility.)

In the context of this passage, why do you think God has designated sex to be acceptable only within a marriage relationship? (The purpose of sex is to allow two bodies to become one. Without the commitment of marriage, sex divides rather than unites. And a Christian who engages in premarital or extramarital sex attempts to unite Jesus with the sinful world, which is not possible. The resulting dissonance then becomes a significant problem for the person.)

STEP

5

Wholly, Wholly, Holy

(Needed: Chalkboard and chalk or newsprint and marker)

Your group members may or may not be experimenting with sex. But all of them are likely to relate to spiritual unfaithfulness. As they begin to discover how closely sexual and spiritual purity are related, their determination to strengthen one area should automatically strengthen the other as well.

Review: Previous sessions have dealt with several aspects of sex. The physical, emotional, and mental considerations of sexual involvements are fairly easy to understand. But the most important aspect of sex may be the most subtle and the most overlooked—the spiritual side of sex. No other human relationship is as important as the husband-wife union. It's the closest thing God can use to help us understand how we are to relate to Him. But if we do not honor our marriage vows to another person whom we can see, hear, touch, and even have sex with, we aren't very likely to remain faithful to our commitment to an invisible God.

The key to both sexual purity and spiritual purity is "holiness"—being "set apart" from any influences that would interfere with the relationship. Wrap up the session by allowing group members to brainstorm ways to be more holy (set apart) in their behaviors toward both God and other people. On a sheet of newsprint or a chalkboard, create two columns—with "God" at the top of one column and "People I Date" above the other. Then challenge group members to come up with as many suggestions as they can to ensure that their own behavior does not fall to the level of the rest of the self-centered world as they relate to God and others. After they compile their lists, see how many of their responses are true of the other column as well. For instance, their responses might include the following:

• Always put the concerns of the other person above your own (also true of God).

• Don't be bothered if people make fun of you for being a Christian (or a virgin).

• Good communication is a key to avoiding problems (prayer is important).

Acknowledge that remaining sexually pure in today's society is not easy. Neither is remaining spiritually pure. But God rewards both. And the sooner we determine to remain faithful, the better off we will be.

Once we "cross the line" in either category, it is hard (and perhaps even painful) to restore the original relationship. It's *possible* (just ask Hosea and Gomer), but a lot of grief can be spared by making the right decisions to begin with and then sticking to those decisions.

Worth the Wait? (Part 4)

(Needed: The list you worked on in Sessions 1-3)

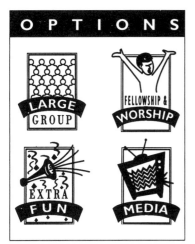

Close by listing additional reasons to save sex for marriage—this time based on a spiritual perspective. Three you might include are:
   • Christians reflect Jesus in *all* of their actions.
   • The faithful-to-one-person sexual relationship is a model for our spiritual relationship to God as well.
   • Sexual promiscuity is a sin that interferes with one's spiritual growth.
Close the session in prayer.

333

THREE OF A KIND

Each of the following "trios" has a common theme. For example, if the grouping were "Combs, saws, prehistoric tigers," the common bond would be "Things with teeth." See how many common themes you can find for the following trios.

1. **Garter, bull, coral**

2. **Money, rivers, snow**

3. *Florida, pianos, songs*

4. Man, peas, flakes

5. DICE, PEEL, BROWN

6. **Ice skates, lawn mowers, windshield wipers**

7. Horns, hens, fries

8. Pigs, bears, wise men

9. **Tree stumps, bathtubs, telephones**

10. Rings, baseball fields, deck of cards

11. Neckties, shoelaces, stomachs

12. Love, service, advantage

13. **Hero, club, submarine**

14. Mercury, Saturn, Galaxy

15. **Murder, pride, school**

MY UNFAITHFUL WIFE:
I Think I'll Keep Her

HOSEA: Hello. My name is Hosea.

PEOPLE: Who?

HOSEA: Hosea. I am a minor prophet … from the Old Testament. God spoke to me …

PEOPLE: That's nice (*yawn*) but we have to go now.

HOSEA: … and told me to marry a loose woman and make babies.

PEOPLE: Well, maybe we *can* hang around a while longer.

HOSEA: This is my wife …

GOMER: I'm his *lovely* wife, Gomer. And no cracks about the name, if you know what's good for you!

HOSEA: Now, dear, don't be rude to the nice people. Just tell your story.

GOMER: OK. We got married.

HOSEA: God *told* me to marry her.

GOMER: And I thought I'd heard 'em all! This guy had a lot to learn about women, and I was just the one to teach him.

HOSEA: We had three lovely children. We named the oldest boy "God Scatters." Our daughter's name is "Not Loved," and our youngest boy is called "Not My People."

GOMER: They're going to have a lot of fun when they start school. Personally, I would have named them "Bob," "Jennifer," and "Hezedekedediah." That's "He-*zed*-e-*ked*-e-*di*-ah." We'd have to have at least *one* biblical sounding name, I guess.

HOSEA: Those weren't *my* choices. God named them. Besides, there are some questions as to whether or not the kids are all mine! Anyway, God …

PEOPLE: Hold it! Back up! What was that?

HOSEA: Well, you see, for a while there I wasn't exactly the only man Gomer was seeing—even after we were married.

PEOPLE: You mean she was a …?

GOMER: Yes. Yes. Whichever name you want to use for it, that's what I was.

PEOPLE: Wasn't that, like, a problem?

GOMER: Of course, it was! For a while I didn't have the respect for Hosea that I should have had. I admit it.

HOSEA: That was the point. God was trying to show our nation something by using the two of us as an example.

GOMER: We were all acting like prostitutes—forsaking God and loving false gods.

PEOPLE: So what happened? It looks like the two of you are back together now.

HOSEA: We are.

GOMER: But it wasn't easy. After I left him and started sleeping around with other guys, I never figured he'd even *want* me again.

HOSEA: But God knew we still loved each other. I had to "buy" her to get her back. But, hey, we're together now and it was well worth the price.

PEOPLE: Did you make her come crawling back to you?

HOSEA: No. I wouldn't have wanted her back if I couldn't have forgiven her.

GOMER: So do you get it?

PEOPLE: Get what?

GOMER: The moral to this story! I'd hate to think Hosea and I went through all this suffering, only to have you nod off while reading through the Minor Prophets and miss the point.

PEOPLE: Of course we know the moral … but, uh, you can tell us anyway.

HOSEA: The moral is that God will not tolerate our unfaithfulness forever, yet He will readily take us back when we repent and turn to Him.

GOMER: And when we go putting other things before Him—especially sexual things—we're nothing more than spiritual prostitutes.

HOSEA: Take it from someone who knows.

GOMER: Hey! I *said* I was sorry.

HOSEA: Yes, dear. I was only joking. The two of us lived happily ever after. As for you listeners, you can too, if you'll only … (*Complete this sentence.*)

Step I

In place of the quiz, form two teams. Whisper the letter "Y" to each person, one at a time—except for two people, one on each team, to whom you whisper the letter "X." Kids must keep their letters a secret. Announce that you're going to have a human tug-of-war (with the rope held only by the two at the front of each line and the rest with arms linked around waists). Reveal that one unknown person on each team (the "X") is a "weak link." That person should participate normally until one team is on the verge of pulling the other across the finish line, when you'll shout, "X!" At that point each "X" should let go of the person (or rope) in front of him or her. Play several rounds, each time whispering "X" to someone on each team. Whichever team is ahead after a predetermined number of rounds is the winner. The winner will be determined by several factors, including the position (front or back) of weak links in each line. Use this to illustrate the fact that you can't be spiritually strong if you have a weak link in one area like sexuality.

Step 5

Bring up four volunteers. Bind each person's wrists with a different material— one with rope, one with masking tape, one with yarn, one with a knot of toilet paper. See who can break the bonds first. Then ask: **Which of these bonds is most like the Bible's sexual rules? Why?** Note that we may feel restricted by God's rules, but He doesn't force us to obey Him. Obedience is to be based on our love for Him and on knowing that His rules are best for us; in that sense, His "bonds" are only as strong as our love for Him and our ability to see His love for us.

Step 2

If you can't rustle up enough people to play the parts of Hosea, Gomer, and the People, you could have kids read the skit silently and then discuss it. Or skip the skit and have kids debate what punishment (if any) people should get for the following sexual sins: (1) living together before marriage; (2) rape; (3) watching an X-rated video; (4) publishing a pornographic magazine; (5) molesting a child. Then compare kids' verdicts with the wrath God shows in the Step 3 study.

Step 4

Guessing who's representing whom won't pose much of a challenge if there aren't many in your group. Instead, display magazine photos of all kinds of people (from little kids to heavy metal musicians to grandmas to well-known politicians). Ask: **Which of these people would you want to stand in for you in the following situations: taking a college entrance exam; applying for a job; asking someone for a date; going to court to fight a traffic ticket?** Why? Then lead into the I Corinthians discussion.

Step 4

Answering questions on each other's behalf may take too long with a large group, and guessing who's who will be tough if kids aren't well acquainted. Try an Elvis impersonators' contest instead. (You may want to get entrants signed up before the session to save time. If your kids aren't familiar with Elvis, choose a different celebrity.) Offer prizes in two categories: Best Vocal Impression and Best Physical Impression (lip-synching to an Elvis song you've brought). Discuss how you think "the king" would feel about being represented by his many imitators. Then move into the I Corinthians discussion about being a representative of Christ.

Step 6

Have teams compete to create and shout out the best group cheers encouraging sexual abstinence before marriage. Examples: "Virgin, virgin, that's OK; virginity goes all the way ... to marriage!" "Gimme an S! Gimme an E! Gimme an S-E-X! But first gimme a V! Gimme an O! Gimme those V-O-W-S!" "Purity, purity—fight, fight, fight! Save it for your wedding night!"

HEARD IT ALL BEFORE

LITTLE BIBLE BACKGROUND

FELLOWSHIP & WORSHIP

Step 1

Kids may resist the idea that they have to talk about "spiritual stuff" to fully understand sexuality. Instead of using the "Three of a Kind" quiz, start with an activity that shows the practical value of knowing about a "dull" subject. Label seven bottles with the following: Na, $NaCl$, $NaHCO_3$, $NaCN$, NaF, $C_2H_2FO_2Na$, Na_2SiO_3. Display the bottles and ask: **All of these contain the element called sodium. Which would be safe to eat or drink?** After kids write down their guesses, reveal that only $NaCl$ (table salt) and $NaHCO_3$ (sodium bicarbonate, or baking soda) would be safe. The rest are dangerous: pure sodium (Na) explodes on contact with water, and the others are poisonous compounds containing things like cyanide and fluorine. **Just as you'd need to know something about chemistry to keep from killing yourself when faced with these choices, we need to know something about spiritual things when faced with sexual choices. Some expressions of sexuality are fine; others are spiritual poison. It takes a little study to know the difference.**

Step 5

Kids may equate holiness with being boring and closeted away from real life. Help them see what it means to be set apart for God's purposes. Have three or four kids roll up their sleeves and dig with plastic spoons in a pail of mud to find a hidden marble. Whoever gets the marble wins. But the prize is a dish of ice cream, which must be eaten with the same spoon used to dig in the dirt. Point out how we "set apart" tools (like eating utensils) used for special jobs. Then pass out clean spoons and give everybody ice cream if possible.

Step 2

Kids may be confused by the Hosea-Gomer story. Instead of using the skit, make a connection between sexual purity and spiritual purity with the following activity. Break the group into pairs. Start reading a story about a guy with an unfaithful girlfriend: **Scott and Caitlin had been going together for over a year. Scott was so in love, always attentive to Caitlin's needs and being a perfect gentleman. But one day he discovered the truth: Caitlin had been sleeping around the whole time. Half the guys in school were laughing at Scott behind his back. That afternoon Scott met Caitlin after school as usual and . . .** Have each pair come up with an ending and share it with the rest of the group. Make the parallel between this story and Israel's (and our) relationship with God.

Step 3

Kids may wonder why it was so important for Israel to maintain its identity. Explain that God had chosen Israel as His people and made a covenant with them. Israel was surrounded by nations that worshiped false gods, and whose religions required everything from prostitution to killing babies as sacrifices. God wanted Israel to do things His way—for the Israelites' own good and to provide an example to the other nations of the way life was *supposed* to be.

Step 1

On index cards, write the following amounts: $50, $500, $5,000, and $50,000. Make at least two cards with each amount, and make enough cards so that each group member will have one. As kids enter, give each person a card. Kids find the other(s) with the same dollar amount and form small groups. Each group must plan a wedding for its oldest member, spending no more than the amount on its card. The oldest member gets to make the final decisions and should explain his or her reasons. Then have each group discuss: **Which kind of marriage is more likely to stay together: one with a cheap wedding or one with an expensive one? If money has nothing to do with it, what do you think keeps husbands and wives faithful to each other?**

Step 6

Bring a guitar or other accompaniment, plus a songbook that includes "I Have Decided to Follow Jesus." Remind kids that sexuality is just one area in which our actions show how we really feel about Jesus and His commands. Sing the existing verses of "I Have Decided"; then have kids make up new ones. Some of these should reflect a commitment to follow Jesus in the sexual choices we make. Example: "Because I love Him, I'll wait for the wedding."

Step 2

To make Repro Resource 8 more appropriate for your group of girls, rewrite it so that Gomer is talking to her neighbors, explaining what happened in her marriage. Have her describe her husband, Hosea, and his attitudes and actions. In rewriting the skit, you can use most of the words already written for Hosea to say.

Step 4

After the discussion, give everyone another slip of paper that has the word "God" written on it. Have each girl write down at least two things God might say about having her as His spokesperson and representative. Ask group members to consider the risk God is taking by asking us to be His representatives. Ask: **How might people learn about God and His sexual standards through you?** Ask volunteers to share some things God might say.

Step 2

Can't do the skit? If you can't get a guy to play Gomer, try this instead. Designate one side of the room as "Perfectly Happy" and the other side as "On a Rampage." Have guys move back and forth between the poles as you read this "love note" addressed to them: **Oh, I miss you so much while I'm away at camp this summer.** (pause) **I can almost see your handsome face —**(pause) **but not quite, because I lost your picture when Chad and I went canoeing.** (pause) **Chad isn't as sweet as you are, of course.** (pause) **But he's better-looking.** (pause) **Still he's not as muscular as some of these guys up here.** (pause) **They keep asking me out, but I say no—**(pause) **unless it's a weekend night.** (pause) **I wish you were here so I could give you a big kiss.** (pause) **But since you aren't, I'll have to settle for Jeremy, Luis, and Jean-Claude.** Then compare guys' feelings to those God might have over the spiritual unfaithfulness of people.

Step 5

The idea of being 100 percent sexually pure and holy may seem hopeless to guys, some of whom have tried unsuccessfully to stamp out sexual thoughts or break habits like masturbation. Encourage them by emphasizing the idea of making steady, step-by-step progress in purity and holiness—getting stronger by resisting temptation and getting forgiveness when they fail. Use the following to illustrate. Have kids try to "broad jump" 15 feet, a task at which they're unlikely to succeed. Then let them jump 15 feet on one foot in as many steps as it takes—a much easier way to get there.

Step 1

Start with Thumb Tag. Form two teams. One team colors its thumbs with blue washable markers; the other team uses red. At your signal, each team tries to leave its thumbprints on the hands of kids on the other team. Kids may touch only hands. After three minutes, examine hands. Anybody left unmarked by the other team wins. Point out that just as kids tried to remain untouched by each other, we need to stay untouched by sexual sin because of the Person whose team we're on.

Step 6

Wrap up the meeting by staging a "wedding reception" mini-party. This can be as simple or as complicated as you like, but it would be good to include a cake, wedding-bell decorations on the walls, and some recorded music in the background. Remind kids that this is a party celebrating the "marriage" of every Christian to Christ.

Step 3

Bring a video camera that has a time-lapse feature. Set it up on a tripod, let it run in time-lapse mode, and see whether kids can sneak into the room, perform a task of your choosing, and sneak out without the camera catching them. The task will depend on the interval of time your camera waits between shots; the longer the interval, the more complex the task should be. After kids try it, play the tape to see whether they escaped detection. Discuss the futility of trying to get away with something sexual without God noticing, which is apparently what the Israelites tried to do in Numbers 25.

Step 6

Wrap up with either of the following. (1) Borrow a wedding video from a couple in your church. Cue it up to the part with the vows, the minister's pronouncement, and the happy couple leaving. Ask: **How is a wedding both very serious and very happy? How is that like becoming a Christian? If we took vows to become Christians, what do you think they might be like? Why do you think we don't?** (2) Listen to and discuss as many wedding songs as you can locate—anything from old standards like "I Love You Truly" to newer favorites like Noel Paul Stookey's "The Wedding Song." What do they say about faithfulness? How much of each song could apply to one's relationship with Christ as well as one's relationship with a husband or wife?

Step 1

Replace Steps 1 and 2 with a shorter opener. Bring enough cans of yellow and blue Play-Doh or other modeling dough so that each person can have a golf-ball-sized lump of one or the other. Form pairs; give one kid in each pair a lump of yellow, and the other kid a lump of blue. Have a race to see which pair, using only the hands holding the dough, is able to first (and thoroughly) combine the yellow and blue to make green. After determining the winner (and awarding a prize if you like), ask kids to separate the colors into yellow and blue again—an impossible assignment. Note that in the same way it's impossible to keep our relationship with God separate from what we do sexually, and vice versa.

Step 4

Skip the representing-each-other activity. Read the 1 Corinthians passage and use the questions following it. In place of Step 5, apply the marriage metaphor with the following wrap-up. Have each person create two time capsules—letters in sealed envelopes. One should be addressed to a future marriage partner, the other to Christ. Both should express whatever promises of faithfulness the person is willing to make at this time. Save the letters and send them to the kids a year from now.

Step 1

Here are some other "three of a kind" groupings you might consider using:
• Candy wrappers, cans, glass bottles (Things for the trash—not the ground)
• TLC, DMC, BBD (Music groups)
• Jordan, Barkley, Ewing (Basketball players)
• Elevator, 20+ floors, people (Things in a high-rise building)
• Tracks, cars, underground (Things associated with a subway)
• Truth, King, Mandela (Great black leaders)
For extra points:
• Umoja, ujima, imani (Things associated with Kwanzaa, the African-American holiday)

Step 5

Distribute paper and pencils. Point out that a famous man, Karl Barth, once described sexuality as the "God-like" in us. Explain that he was talking about those positive "sexy feelings" which are given by God and are most appealing in our personalities. These can be used to bring joy to others and glory to God. Have each group member write a list of ten things God would describe as "sexy" about him or her. However, group members may name only one item that concerns their outward appearance. Afterward, ask for volunteers to read what they've written. Then discuss the areas in our lives in which holiness and sexuality converge. Emphasize that sexuality is not simply "acts of sex," but a pursuit to obtain a "Christ-likeness" within.

Step 2
The Hosea-Gomer story may go over the heads of younger kids. Instead, make the point that you can't separate your relationship with God from sexual relationships, pretending that one doesn't affect the other. Bring a doll house with furnishings (borrow one from a young girl or an older woman who's into collectibles). Cover the opening to one of the rooms with paper, so that kids can't see it. Let kids admire the other rooms. Then tear off the paper and reveal the last room—which you've filled with "gross" stuff like rubber bugs. Use this as an illustration of how some people let God clean up every "room" of their lives except the one involving sexuality.

Step 5
Younger kids will have a tough time coming up with ways to be holy. Skip the two-column approach and ask questions like these to help them brainstorm ways to be "set apart": **If you had a computer, what would you want to keep it away from so that you could really use it?** (Computer viruses, heat, cold, water, lightning storms, clumsy people, etc.) **If you had a car, what would you keep it away from so you could use it?** (Rust, vandals, thieves, accidents, potholes, bad gasoline, etc.) **What might God want to keep you away from so that He can really use you?** (People who tell you not to believe in Him, daydreams or guilt feelings that preoccupy you all the time, hobbies that keep you too busy, dangers that might hurt you, etc.) **What sexual temptations and activities might God want to "set us apart" from so that He can really use us?** (Fantasies that keep us from thinking about Him, habits that make us feel too guilty to talk to Him, videos and magazines that encourage those fantasies and habits, sexual relationships that draw us away from Him, etc.)

Step 4
Follow the I Corinthians passage by discussing the following imaginary situation. **A new NC-17 movie has just come to town. It's called _The Secret Life of Jesus_, and it portrays Jesus as having sexual encounters with most of the women who followed Him. The movie's most notorious scene shows Jesus and His disciples going into a brothel and having sex with prostitutes. Most people in your church are angry about the movie, but not sure what to do about it. How would you feel about such a movie? Why? What would you want to do about it? How is this like the I Corinthians passage? If you were God, what might you want to do about Christians who, through sexual immorality, "take the members of Christ and unite them with a prostitute"?**

Step 5
Challenge kids to go beyond discussing holiness and to make a personal commitment. Bring copies of the traditional wedding ceremony (your pastor should have it) and pass them out. Using this as a model (or departing from it if kids want to), have group members write "wedding vows" expressing their commitment to be faithful to Jesus. Each person should write one or two sentences. Then put the vows together, photocopy them, and read them aloud as a group. Encourage kids to take the copies with them and to look at them again this week.

Date Used:

Approx.
Time

Step 1: Common Bonds _____
o Extra Action
o Heard It All Before
o Fellowship & Worship
o Extra Fun
o Short Meeting Time
o Urban
Things needed:

Step 2: Don't Take ... _____
o Small Group
o Little Bible Background
o Mostly Girls
o Mostly Guys
o Combined Junior High/High School
Things needed:

Step 3: The Cozbi Show _____
o Little Bible Background
o Media
Things needed:

Step 4: Representatives _____
o Small Group
o Large Group
o Mostly Girls
o Short Meeting Time
o Extra Challenge
Things needed:

Step 5: Wholly, Wholly ... _____
o Extra Action
o Heard It All Before
o Mostly Guys
o Urban
o Combined Junior High/High School
o Extra Challenge
Things needed:

Step 6: Worth the Wait ... _____
o Large Group
o Fellowship & Worship
o Extra Fun
o Media
Things needed:

5 Being Sexual without Being Sinful

YOUR GOALS FOR THIS SESSION:

Choose one or more

☐ To help kids see that, while being "sexual" is a natural part of life, there are certain limits that should be self-imposed at this point in their lives.

☐ To help kids understand that no matter how much they know about sex, it's what they do about it that matters most.

☐ To help kids who are already guilty of sexual sins experience complete forgiveness and get a new start.

☐ Other _____

Your Bible Base:

1 Kings 11:1-13
Proverbs 7:6-27
John 8:1-11

Object Lesson

(Needed: A variety of objects of assorted shapes, sizes, and weights)

Have group members sit in a large circle and pass an object (like a tennis ball) from person to person. Explain that if someone drops the object, he or she is out. If the drop occurs during a hand-off from one person to the next, both people are out. When this happens, tighten the circle and continue playing with the remaining people. As group members begin to get a bit bored (or smug) from handling the single item, begin another item (like a bowling ball) going in the opposite direction. At regular intervals, keep adding new objects (a single hair, a lawn chair, an egg, etc.).

Group members should soon discover that while any of these things are easily managed individually, they can cause significant problems when combined or when they appear unexpectedly. Trying to deal with sexual issues is somewhat similar. As young people try to deal with all the aspects of sexuality—physical, emotional, mental, and spiritual—the challenge may seem overwhelming. The purpose of this session is to help your young people put together a practical plan for how to deal with the sexual issues in their lives.

Let's Make a Deal

(Needed: A mixture of inexpensive "gift" items, both gag gifts and nice ones)

Call for some volunteers and let them participate in a quick game of "Let's Make a Deal." Provide one person with an attractively wrapped item and see if he or she would be willing to trade for what's "behind the curtain" (or "in the sack," "under the table," etc.). If the person trades, offer the item he or she gives up to someone else who will then have similar options.

In each case, make sure to provide the person with his or her best possible choice *to begin with* (whether or not he or she can even tell what the item is at the time). Anyone who trades should unknowingly be trading down in value. Have some fun with creative gag gifts. But later, at an appropriate time, make a serious point: A person's virginity is a very special thing that should not be traded (or given) away lightly. It is a thing of value that should be cherished. Given in the context of marriage, it is replaced with intimacy, and genuine love can continue to grow. Given prior to marriage, however, it is lost forever. Only too late do many people discover that the exchange of their virginity for a short-lived "loving" relationship is a bad trade.

STEP 3

Opinion Poll

(Needed: Calculator)

Ask the following questions and have group members respond. Record their answers and come up with an average for each question. You will probably need a calculator.

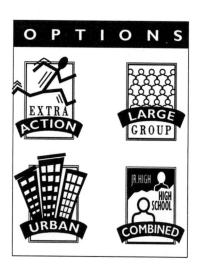

• **What percent of people your age do you think are unaware of how sex works—the actual physical act of sexual intercourse?**

• **What percent do you think don't really know about the physical risks such as pregnancy, AIDS, other sexually transmitted diseases, and so forth?**

• **What percent would you say, as they begin to feel sexual urges, really take into account the feelings of the other person as much as their own?**

• **What percent would you say continue a lasting relationship with the first person they have sex with?**

• **What percent do you think look beyond the actual sexual act and anticipate the emotions that are likely to be felt afterward—confusion, worry, guilt, shame, uncertainty, etc.?**

• **What percent would you say think about sex too much?**

• **What percent do you think have some kind of personal, religious, or moral standard that prevents them from participating in sex?**

• **Of the people you know who have had sex, what percent would you say are more satisfied because they did?**

• **Of the people you know who have had sex, what percent would you say were pretty much aware of most of the physical, emotional, mental, and spiritual aspects of sex, yet went ahead and became sexually active anyway?**

Discuss the results of your opinion poll. Are any of the answers surprising or shocking? Do any of them need to be challenged? Were any of your group members surprised by any of the others' answers?

Explain that when it comes to dealing with sex, most people are probably knowledgeable of the "how-to" part. Many are also aware of the risks and potential consequences. Yet in spite of all the knowledge and the awareness, they go ahead and have sex.

Ask: **Why do you think so many people choose to have sex in spite of all they know?** (They get caught up in the heat of the moment. They are so eager to experience the feeling that they ignore the facts. They are swayed more by someone they like than by their own convictions.)

STEP

4

Like an Ox Going to the Slaughter

(Needed: Bibles)

OPTIONS

LITTLE BIBLE BACKGROUND

MOSTLY GIRLS

MOSTLY GUYS

SHORT MEETING TIME

JR.HIGH HIGH SCHOOL COMBINED

Call for one male and one female volunteer (people involved in drama, if possible). Explain that you are going to narrate a passage and you want them to pantomime the action of the script. It begins with the guy, and the girl comes in soon thereafter.

Read aloud Proverbs 7:6-23, giving your actors time to respond to what you are reading and allowing them to create the proper motions and facial expressions. After you have finished reading the passage, let your actors take a bow. But then finish by reading verses 24-27. Ask: **Do you think this is an accurate portrayal of young men who allow themselves to be seduced by more "experienced" women?**

Explain that this advice was given by Solomon. Then see how much your group members can recall about Solomon. They should be aware that he:

• was the wisest man of his time (I Kings 10:23).
• was the wealthiest man of his time.
• was the person chosen by God to build the temple.
• had good common sense in addition to "smartness" (as attested by

his handling of the "Whose child is it?" case [I Kings 3:16-28] and his encounter with the Queen of Sheba [I Kings 10:1-13]).

If you read through I Kings 10:14-29 and see everything Solomon had, it's hard to imagine that *anything* could destroy such an empire of wealth and wisdom that he had accumulated. Yet something did.

Have group members read I Kings 11:1-13. Then discuss: **Do you know what a "concubine" is?** (A woman who was lawfully married to a man, yet didn't have the full title or benefits of a regular wife. Concubines could be sent away and their children excluded from an inheritance by simply awarding them a small gift.)

Was it wrong for Solomon to have concubines? (Even though God had established a monogamous husband-wife relationship, many men during Old Testament times had more than one wife, including concubines. This was never God's ideal.)

What was Solomon's real problem? (He was attracted by women whom God had specifically forbidden him to get involved with.)

Do you think God's restrictions were unreasonable? (Not at all. Solomon fell right into the trap that God had warned about. He abandoned his faith in God—the very thing that had allowed him to accumulate his wealth and wisdom—and began to worship the gods of his many wives. The worship of some of these gods even included sacrificing children to them, so this was no small offense.)

Why was Solomon's sin so significant? (For one thing, it shows the power of sex to cause an otherwise intelligent person to forsake everything he has to get more and more involved in sensual pleasures. For another, since Solomon was an influential and powerful person, he established the worship of these foreign gods in his own land—exposing the whole nation to spiritual, as well as physical, prostitution.)

What was the result of Solomon's sexual entanglements? (The united kingdom of Saul and David would be divided. Solomon's own son would not inherit the power and influence that Solomon had accumulated. And perhaps worst of all, Solomon would be remembered more for his final failure than for all of his unprecedented accomplishments.)

Point out that if Solomon could be brought to ruin by not being able to control his sexual activities, none of us is immune.

Too Late to Wait?

(Needed: Bibles, pens, copies of Repro Resource 9)

Explain: **We need to be practical in our approach to sex. We need to know about all the aspects of sex—physical, emotional, mental, and spiritual. But it takes more than knowing about these things. We must act on what we know. As difficult as it might be, we need to use common sense. For example, try to determine what practical, commonsense options are appropriate in each of the following situations:**

(1) After only three dates, Sean and Francis have gone from hand holding to some pretty serious fondling of each other.

(2) Sally really likes Dave, but doesn't want to have sex. Dave likes Sally too, but he really wants to have sex.

(3) Ken and Debbie haven't yet gone "all the way," but they've done a lot more than Debbie is comfortable with.

(4) Bob and Lisa have gone all the way. But now they realize they can't handle the pressure that sexual activity creates, and they don't know what to do.

Group members should see that in many of these cases, the options boil down to one of two. The people involved must either: (1) commit to slowing down and finding non-sexual things to do together, or (2) stop dating altogether. Otherwise, the escalation of sexual desire and experimentation can get out of control. Saving sex "until the time is right" never works unless the "right time" is mutually determined to be "on our wedding night." To ignore the practical outcomes of sexual feelings and decisions is to invite temptation and trouble.

Hand out copies of "Any Questions?" (Repro Resource 9). This sheet will encourage group members to raise any questions that may not have been dealt with yet. If time permits, deal with their questions at this time. If not, schedule a discussion at a later meeting. But remember that the sooner your young people find good answers to their questions, the sooner they will be able to make wise decisions regarding their sexual behavior.

One question that group members may be a little hesitant to ask is: "What if it's too late for me to remain a virgin? What if I've already gone too far?" In response, read aloud John 8:1-11. It should need little comment. But two things are very clear:

(1) *Sexual sin can and will be forgiven.* God understands our strong feelings. He doesn't want one sin to separate us from Him forever. So if sexual sin has taken place—regardless of the magnitude—we should confess it to Him and experience His full forgiveness.

(2) *Sexual sin must be eliminated.* God forgives our "sins of passion," yet He is serious about our not allowing such behavior to become a lifestyle. When we experience His freeing forgiveness, we should, from that point on, try to avoid any further entanglements with sin.

Provide a time of silent prayer so group members can confess any such recent sins. Then challenge them not to overlook the importance of a fresh start. You might also let them know that you are available at any time to help them think through and talk through any hard decisions they need to make.

STEP
6

Worth the Wait? (Part 5)

(Needed: Copies of Repro Resource 10, copies of the list you worked on in Sessions 1-4)

Hand out copies of "Worth the Wait? Definitely!" (Repro Resource 10), as well as copies of the list your group has compiled. Challenge group members to keep the list(s) in a place where they will be seen frequently. And encourage your young people to continue to add to them. As they think of new reasons to save sex for marriage, let them share their observations at future meetings and make this an ongoing project.

[Optional ending: If any time remains, have a few more volunteers play "Let's Make a Deal." Because of the first game, the tendency of your group members should be to hold on to what you give them the first time. But this time if anyone is willing to trade, make sure each successive swap is better than the previous one. The first lesson was that virginity should not be quickly traded away. But use this final demonstration to show that God never expects us to give up something without providing us with something better. When we "take a pass" on the opportunities for sexual encounters that come our way, we can experience His full peace, love, joy, and more. In addition, we have clean consciences, and can look forward to eternal rewards. "Sacrificing" for God is never a bad trade when we look at the long-term results.]

ANY QUESTIONS?

Most people have a lot of questions about sex. Some answers are found very quickly.
Other answers seem to escape us for a long time. You may have found answers to many of
your sexual questions, but perhaps you're still hoping to have a question or two answered.
Look over the questions below and circle any that you're not sure you know how to answer.
Also add any questions that you have, but that you haven't gotten around to asking yet.

IF I DON'T HAVE THE SAME SEXUAL URGES THAT SOME OF MY FRIENDS TALK
ABOUT, AM I ABNORMAL?

IF I'VE ALREADY GOTTEN INVOLVED SEXUALLY, ISN'T IT TOO LATE TO WORRY
ABOUT HOW I ACT FROM NOW ON?

IF I RULE OUT SEX AS AN OPTION, HOW CAN I PROVE THAT I LOVE SOMEONE?

IF I SAVE SEX UNTIL MY WEDDING NIGHT, HOW WILL I KNOW WHAT TO DO?

HOW DO I HANDLE THE PRESSURE BEING PUT ON ME TO HAVE SEX—WITH-
OUT COMPLETELY DESTROYING THE RELATIONSHIP?

WHAT IF SOMEONE OF THE SAME GENDER SEEMS ATTRACTED TO ME?

_____

_____

_____

WORTH THE WAIT? DEFINITELY!

As a relatively normal teenager, you're going to hear a few "logical" reasons from some of your friends why it's "perfectly OK" to go ahead and have sex whenever you're ready. But here's a list of twelve even better reasons why you should save sex for marriage. (And this is just a starter list. Feel free to add other reasons as you think of them.) The next time you start feeling a little pressure to give in, consult this list (and if possible, also consult a good Christian friend or counselor).

Why Should We Save Sex for *Marriage?*

1. All risk of premarital pregnancy (and its many complications) is eliminated.

2. Any risk of the sexually transmitted HIV (AIDS) virus disappears.

3. The risk of other sexually transmitted diseases (syphilis, gonorrhea, etc.) is gone.

4. We never have to worry about "getting caught." Rather than living with guilt, shame, and other horrible feelings, we can eventually experience the full pleasure of sex with complete peace of mind.

5. We offer our future spouses a first-ever, one-of-a-kind experience, and give him or her complete loyalty.

6. When sexual entanglements are removed, our current relationships will be stronger (and probably longer).

7. We find much more efficient uses for our mental time and energy, rather than thinking so much about our sexual encounters.

8. Our priorities remain clear and we are able to focus better on schoolwork, jobs, and other important areas of life.

9. Abstinence is a source of creative power. Rather than allowing lust to overwhelm us and be channeled through sexual encounters, our powerful emotions can be expressed more appropriately through songs, poems, plays, and so forth.

10. Christians reflect Jesus in all of their actions. Sexual unions make us (and Him) look particularly bad.

11. The one-to-one sexual relationship in the context of a loving and committed marriage is a model for our spiritual relationship with God.

12. We cannot grow spiritually if we have recurring sexual sin in our lives.

Step 3

In place of the survey, play "Time Bomb." Have kids stand in a circle. Set a wind-up kitchen timer on one minute or so and put it in a lunchbox or similar container. Kids must pass the "bomb" around the circle as quickly as they can; whoever's touching it when it goes off is out. Repeat until you've eliminated all of the kids. (If your group is too large for this, just have five or six kids play the game while the rest of the group watches. Either way, play until all participants are out.) Ask how waiting for the bomb to go off is like having premarital sex despite the risks. Then talk about how kids take risks sexually even when they supposedly know what's going on, thinking the consequences (pregnancy, AIDS, etc.) won't happen to them.

Step 5

Have several volunteers compete in a 50-yard dash. The winner is the first person who crosses the finish line *and* reaches a complete stop within five feet of crossing the line. Have half the non-runners watch the finish line and half watch the "stop" line. After declaring a winner, discuss how hard it was to run as fast as you could, yet try to stop quickly. Tie this into the fact that the further you go sexually, the tougher it is to stop.

Step 1

Since a small group can't sit in a large circle, replace the object pass with a "driver's test." Have kids sit in a row, side by side, with a few feet between chairs. Sit behind kids, as if they were in the front seat of a car and you were in the back. Then give instructions (turn right, accelerate, stop, etc.). Kids respond with hand signals, verbal "vrooms" and screeches, etc. But they must do the *opposite* of what you tell them. Anyone who doesn't do the opposite is out. Then discuss the fact that some kids who know the sexual "rules of the road" from the Bible still insist on doing the opposite.

Step 5

Kids may be reluctant to hand in their sexual questions on the Repro Resource, knowing you probably can guess whose sheet is whose. Try these approaches: (1) Cut the questions from the sheet; give a set to each person. Pass around a box with a slot in the top and let kids put in any of the questions that interest them (sort of a secret ballot). (2) For additional questions, give each person a turn at a typewriter to type a question and put it in the question box (so that handwriting won't be recognizable).

Step 2

To allow more group members to participate, replace "Let's Make a Deal" with the following. Before the session, cut two-inch-square samples of all sorts of gift wrap that's meant for specific occasions. Cut each square so that it's hard to tell what the whole pattern is. Glue each sample to an index card and write a number on the card. Display the cards on the walls around your meeting place. Give each person paper and pencil to record his or her guess as to what occasion each type of paper is for. The one with the most correct guesses wins. Then show the group the larger pieces of wrap that you cut the samples from so that they can see the whole pattern. Use this to illustrate two points: (1) just as each type of wrap was for one special occasion, so is sex (the occasion being marriage); and (2) when we're concentrating on a small part of the pattern (whether it's wrapping paper or the right-now urgency we feel about sex at a given moment), it's hard to see the big picture.

Step 3

Recording individual survey responses and averaging them may take too long in a large group. Instead, mark percentages from 0 to 100 (in increments of 10) on a roll of butcher paper and hang it along one wall. Have kids respond to each question by standing under the number that reflects their answer. Draw a star on the paper where most of the kids are bunched (or make a rough visual estimate of the average and draw the star there). Have kids sit down so they can see the stars and discuss their answers.

Step 5

Some kids may have heard many times that God forgives all kinds of sins, but can't bring themselves to believe that He'll forgive theirs. Have small groups make "wanted" posters for Rahab (wanted for prostitution—see Joshua 2 and Hebrews 11:31); David (wanted for adultery and conspiracy to commit murder—see II Samuel 11); Moses (wanted for murder—see Exodus 2:11-15); Paul (wanted as Saul for conspiracy to commit murder—see Acts 7:54-8:1). Discuss what happened to these people and how God forgave and used them despite "big-time" sins, sexual and otherwise. Explain that God is ready to forgive us if we repent. We're "wanted" by Him for a loving, personal relationship.

Step 6

Try one more time to get jaded kids thinking with "Recorder Roulette." Before the session, record statements like these on audio tape with a five-second pause after each: "Boy, are you lucky—only God knows what you did." "You figured sex was okay because you were in love, but you just got dumped." "Sorry, you've tested HIV-positive." "Nobody got pregnant this time." "Ready or not, the two of you are going to have a baby." "The good news: It's not AIDS. The bad news: It's herpes." At this point in the session, explain that premarital sex is like Russian roulette—it's always risky. Have volunteers, posing as sexually active kids, come up one at a time to push the "play" button on the recorder to hear the results of their latest encounter. Push the "stop" button after each statement. Then discuss the "It'll-never-happen-to-me" myth.

Step 4

Instead of the Solomon story, try something simpler: James 1:21-25. Use questions like these to spark discussion: **When you see the phrase "moral filth," what do you think of?** (We may think of sexual sin, but other sins qualify, too.) **What are some sexual "evils" that are "prevalent" (vs. 21) today? How common do you think these things are among Christian teenagers? Why? Why would someone listen to God's instructions about sex, yet do nothing about them? If people's sexual sins somehow showed on their faces, what do you think most kids would see in the mirror? What's the difference between hearing a sermon and looking "intently into the perfect law"? How could we keep from forgetting what we've heard here about sex?**

Step 5

Explain the background of John 8:1-11, the story of the woman caught in adultery. Note that both the man and the woman had sinned; but the religious leaders must have let the man escape. They also misquoted the Old Testament law; execution had to be by stoning only if the woman was a virgin and was engaged, and in that case both the man and woman were to be executed. The leaders asked Jesus a trick question, trying to get Him in trouble with Roman law (the Romans didn't let the Jewish people perform executions) or Jewish law. Note also that Jesus didn't just say "That's OK" to the woman; He told her to stop sinning.

Step 1

Before the session, get a jigsaw puzzle with twenty-five to fifty pieces. Put it together on a sheet of stiff cardboard. Put another piece of cardboard on top of it and turn the whole thing over. Write the names of group members all over the back of the puzzle, breaking names up (half a name on one piece, half on another). Repeat names as often as needed to fill up the puzzle. Then take the puzzle apart and put it in the box. At the meeting, have kids put the puzzle together, using only the names for reference. Then discuss how we often feel alone in facing sexual pressure, but need to remember that (1) we all face similar problems, (2) we can pray for and encourage each other, and (3) we can remember we're not the only ones who believe in saving sex for marriage.

Step 6

Read Romans 11:33–12:1. Discuss what it means to offer our bodies as living sacrifices. Ask: **Why are we to do this?** (As worship, because of God's greatness described in 11:33-36.) Have each person cut a human figure from a sheet of paper. As kids do so, they should think about their willingness to give their bodies to God for His use. Let them show the degree of their willingness by having them place (or not place) their cutout figures in a "recycling bin" (any container that you provide). Point out that God wants not just our knees for kneeling or our mouths for singing, but all of us—including our sexuality.

MOSTLY GIRLS

MOSTLY GUYS

EXTRA FUN

Step 4

Instead of using a guy-girl skit for Proverbs 7:6-23, ask two girls to present the passage. Have one read the verses as a narrator/ observer from the window of her house; have the other pantomime the actions of the woman described in verses 10-23. Finish the presentation by reading aloud verses 24-27.

Step 5

After discussing the four situations, ask your group members to talk about the pressure they feel to have sex, and/or to keep talking about whether you have or will have sex. Ask: **Where is this pressure coming from?** Work together as a group to make a list of the possible sources of the pressure. Include on the list a boyfriend, guy friends, girl friends, the media, and things you read. Talk about why it might be important to someone to give in to these pressures.

Step 4

Pantomiming the Proverbs "seduction" will be either impossible or hard to take seriously if you have no girls; if you have just one or two girls, they may feel unfairly singled out. Instead, just take turns reading the passage. Then ask questions that help guys update the passage to include situations they face today: **Out of all the cases in which teenagers have sex before marriage these days, what percentage do you think are "started" by the girl? By the guy? In what percentage do the guy and girl have equal responsibility? If most girls aren't giving guys this kind of invitation, why do so many guys think they're entitled to have sex? In what ways are some movies, TV shows, ads, and music giving guys the same message as the woman in this passage? How could premarital sex cost you your life** (vs. 23) **physically? Emotionally? Spiritually?**

Step 6

Guys may feel they won't become real men until they go through the "rite of passage" of having sex. Form small groups and have them come up with different ways of "proving" one's manhood without having sex. Ideas could be serious or funny. To help them along, ask: **What if people in our culture felt you weren't a real man until you changed a diaper? Until you led someone to accept Jesus? Until you lifted your father over your head?** You may want to point out that Jesus was a real man—and He never had sex.

Step 1

Bring two identical, fairly complex board or card games that few if any kids in your group are familiar with. Form two teams. Half the kids on each team get to see the instructions but not play; the other half get to play but not see the instructions. Players may ask yes-or-no questions to try to discover the rules from the non-players. The first team to complete a round of the game, following the rules, wins. (You'll need a judge, someone who knows the game, to watch each team to make sure the rules are followed.) Tie this into the fact that one has to know the rules and follow them to play the game. It's not enough to just know rules or just fool around with the game pieces. Similarly, we need to know God's sexual instructions and follow them—not just know them and ignore them.

Step 6

Have a mustard-eating contest. Set out three large bowls of the stuff and ask for volunteers (or get volunteers before they know what they'll be eating). Contestants must keep their hands behind them and use only their mouths. Allow two minutes; chances are that kids won't be able to eat much without getting really tired of it. After rewarding the winner (perhaps with a jar of mustard), ask how contestants felt after the first mouthful or so. Then note that sex, like mustard, is great in the right context (sex in marriage, mustard on a hot dog). Out of context, though, it can be boring and even unpleasant. Wrap up by serving hot dogs—with mustard.

MEDIA

Step 2
Instead of playing "Let's Make a Deal," watch coming attractions from the beginning of a couple of movie videotapes. Analyze how the clips were arranged to make the movie look more exciting, scarier, or funnier than it might really be. If anyone has seen the movie, ask how accurate the coming attractions are. What was left out? Have kids been disappointed by any movies after seeing ads or clips? Compare this to the "buildup" that premarital sex is given on TV and in movies—versus the reality of giving up one's virginity.

Step 6
Bring a rap accompaniment tape. Form six groups or pairs. Assign each group or pair to rewrite two of the twelve reasons on Repro Resource 10 so that they become phrases in "The Let-It-Wait Rap." Then have kids take turns performing their parts of the rap for each other. Consider having the whole group perform the rap at a later date for your entire church or for your junior high group.
Here are a few ideas to get you started:
"Yo! Listen everybody to something great—
Twelve hip reasons to let it wait
'Til you're married—yeah, that's the plan
It's God's design for every woman and man
Reason one is plain to see
It'll keep you from unwanted pregnancy."

SHORT MEETING TIME

Step I
Replace Steps I and 2 with a short opener. Before the session, tape "Wet Paint" signs all over your meeting place. Plant one or two group members in the room who have paint on their hands or faces. Make sure your helpers show off the paint as kids enter. See who ignores the evidence and touches the paint. Use this example of evidence-ignoring to lead into the Step 3 survey. Instead of recording and averaging survey responses, save time by asking for one response to each question and letting others disagree during discussion if they wish.

Step 4
For a shorter Bible study, see either the "Combined Junior High/High School" option or the "Little Bible Background" option. In Step 5, break into four small groups or pairs. Have each group or pair discuss just one of the situations (Sean and Francis, etc.) and give a one-minute report to the other groups.

URBAN

Step 2
Conclude this step with a short study of one or more of Jesus' parables. Point out that virginity is as much a beauty to God as sex during marriage. Both are traits of the kingdom of God. As such, some of the parables of Jesus can adequately describe the validity and beauty of virginity. Among the parables you might consider using:
• The Pearl of Great Price (Matthew 13:45, 46)
• The Hidden Treasure (Matthew 13:44)
• The Mustard Seed (Matthew 13:31, 32).

Step 3
Here are some alternate questions you can use to make the survey more urban-specific.
• **What percent of the people in this group would you say are having sex?**
• **What percent of your peers would (or do) go to the school nurse for condoms?**
• **How many teenagers do you know who have died from AIDS?**
• **How many of your peers have a child already?**
• **What percent of the kids in your high school would you say are actively gay?**
• **What one thing would reduce teenage pregnancy forever?**
• **How many of your peers have a sexual disease, but continue to have sex?**
• **What percent of your peers would approve of the arm-implant method to prevent young ladies from becoming pregnant for five years?**
• **What percent of the kids in your school are virgins and proud of it?**
These aren't all "percentage" questions, so you'll have to adjust the activity accordingly.

Step 3

Younger kids may find it hard to answer the survey questions. Instead, turn them into a mystery to be solved. Before the session, write the following five clues on separate slips of paper: "Fred knows how the physical part of sex works." "Fred knows the physical risks such as pregnancy, AIDS, etc." "Fred knows that people often feel guilty, worried, and ashamed after having premarital sex." "Fred believes it's wrong to have premarital sex." "Fred knows kids who have had sex and who then split up." Hide the clues throughout your meeting place (don't make them too tough to find). Say: **Fred is a teenager who recently started having sex. Why he decided that is a mystery. Look around and see if you can find some written clues that might help us solve the mystery.** After kids find and read the clues aloud, point out that there must be a missing clue; otherwise, why would Fred ignore everything he knows and believes? Lead into the discussion in the last two paragraphs of Step 3.

Step 4

Kids may be confused by the example of Solomon, not to mention his concubines. Instead, study the temptation of Jesus (Matthew 4:1-11). Ask what appeals the devil used (physical appetite; testing God by taking unnecessary risks; getting power and recognition). **How does sexual temptation appeal to us in the same way?** (By using our normal sexual desires; by convincing us that we won't have to suffer consequences; by offering power over people by making them "conquests," giving us recognition as being sexy or grown up, etc.) Encourage kids to remember that the same enemy who tempted Jesus is behind our temptation today.

Step 1

If the basic first two steps aren't brain-oriented enough for your group, substitute the following. Before the session, cut from newspapers and magazines a few dozen "cents-off" coupons for groceries, fast food, household items, etc. Put them face down on a table in your meeting place. To start the session, have several kids come up one at a time and take two coupons each. Each person must explain in one minute why one of the coupons he or she drew is objectively more valuable than the other. Some choices may be easy, but many won't. For example, is it better to get 75 cents off a bottle of aspirin or 25 cents off a candy bar? What if you never have headaches, or you're on a diet? Challenge kids' choices and allow other group members to do so. Then point out the many factors involved in seeing the real value of one coupon over the other. In the same way, the pleasure of sex now may seem more valuable than the rightness of sex postponed—but it's a lot more complicated than that.

Step 6

Using the Repro Resource, have kids rank the twelve reasons to show which are most important and convincing to them personally. For example, someone who is most concerned with the risk of AIDS and not at all with the creative power of abstinence might write a "1" by #2 and a "12" by #9. Share results as kids are willing.

Date Used:

Approx.
Time

Step 1: Object Lesson _____
o Small Group
o Fellowship & Worship
o Extra Fun
o Short Meeting Time
o Extra Challenge
Things needed:

Step 2: Let's Make a Deal _____
o Large Group
o Media
o Urban
Things needed:

Step 3: Opinion Poll _____
o Extra Action
o Large Group
o Urban
o Combined Junior High/High School
Things needed:

Step 4: Like an Ox ... _____
o Little Bible Background
o Mostly Girls
o Mostly Guys
o Short Meeting Time
o Combined Junior High/High School
Things needed:

Step 5: Too Late to Wait? _____
o Extra Action
o Small Group
o Heard It All Before
o Little Bible Background
o Mostly Girls
Things needed:

Step 6: Worth the Wait ... _____
o Heard It All Before
o Fellowship & Worship
o Mostly Guys
o Extra Fun
o Media
o Extra Challenge
Things needed:

Custom Curriculum Critique

Please take a moment to fill out this evaluation form, rip it out, fold it, tape it, and send it back to us. This will help us continue to customize products for you. Thanks!

1. Overall, please give this *Custom Curriculum* course (*Hormone Helper*) a grade in terms of how well it worked for you. (A=excellent; B=above average; C=average; D=below average; F=failure) Circle one.

   A   B   C   D   F

2. Now assign a grade to each part of this curriculum that you used.

a. Upfront article	A	B	C	D	F	Didn't use
b. Publicity/Clip art	A	B	C	D	F	Didn't use
c. Repro Resource Sheets	A	B	C	D	F	Didn't use
d. Session 1	A	B	C	D	F	Didn't use
e. Session 2	A	B	C	D	F	Didn't use
f. Session 3	A	B	C	D	F	Didn't use
g. Session 4	A	B	C	D	F	Didn't use
h. Session 5	A	B	C	D	F	Didn't use

3. How helpful were the options?
   - ❏ Very helpful   ❏ Not too helpful
   - ❏ Somewhat helpful   ❏ Not at all helpful

4. Rate the amount of options:
   - ❏ Too many
   - ❏ About the right amount
   - ❏ Too few

5. Tell us how often you used each type of option (4=Always; 3=Sometimes; 2=Seldom; 1=Never)

	4	3	2	1
Extra Action	❏	❏	❏	❏
Combined Jr. High/High School	❏	❏	❏	❏
Urban	❏	❏	❏	❏
Small Group	❏	❏	❏	❏
Large Group	❏	❏	❏	❏
Extra Fun	❏	❏	❏	❏
Heard It All Before	❏	❏	❏	❏
Little Bible Background	❏	❏	❏	❏
Short Meeting Time	❏	❏	❏	❏
Fellowship and Worship	❏	❏	❏	❏
Mostly Guys	❏	❏	❏	❏
Mostly Girls	❏	❏	❏	❏
Media	❏	❏	❏	❏
Extra Challenge (High School only)	❏	❏	❏	❏
Sixth Grade (Jr. High only)	❏	❏	❏	❏

6. What did you like best about this course?

7. What suggestions do you have for improving *Custom Curriculum*?

8. Other topics you'd like to see covered in this series:

9. Are you?
  ❑ Full time paid youthworker
  ❑ Part time paid youthworker
  ❑ Volunteer youthworker

10. When did you use *Custom Curriculum*?
  ❑ Sunday School   ❑ Small Group
  ❑ Youth Group   ❑ Retreat
  ❑ Other _____

11. What grades did you use it with? _____

12. How many kids used the curriculum in an average week? _____

13. What's the approximate attendance of your entire Sunday school program (Nursery through Adult)? _____

14. If you would like information on other *Custom Curriculum* courses, or other youth products from David C. Cook, please fill out the following:

Name: _____
Church Name: _____
Address: _____
_____
Phone: (____) _____

Thank you!